Kris Zogg

five

5

SMOOTH
STONES

DISCOVERING

THE PATH TO

WHOLENESS OF SOUL

D1510914

Five Smooth Stones

Tom Nelson, Five Smooth Stones

ISBN 1-929478-29-1

Cross Training Publishing
317 West Second Street
Grand Island, NE 68801
(308) 384-5762

Copyright © 2001 by Cross Training Publishing

All rights reserved. No part of this book may be reproduced without
written permission from the publisher, except by a reviewer who may
quote brief passages in a review; nor may any part of this book be
reproduced, stored in a retrieval system or transmitted in any form or
other without written permission from the publisher.

This book is manufactured in the United States of America.

Library of Congress Cataloging in Publication Data in Progress.

Published by Cross Training Publishing,
317 West Second Street
Grand Island, NE 68801

For more information about the author for speaking engagements:
Tom Nelson at tomn@ccefc.org

DEDICATION

This book is dedicated to Delight Nelson who has consistently modeled an authentic spirituality and who from my earliest memories has guided me down a path to true wholeness of soul. I am eternally grateful to call you mom.

ACKNOWLEDGEMENTS

I want to especially thank my bride Liz who has and continues to be the love of my life. Her threads of insight and encouragement are woven into the fabric of my soul as well as this book.

A special thanks to Bill and Paula Nyman for picking up the basin and towel on this project. My deepest appreciation to Gordon Thiessen and Cross Training Publishing for their commitment to excellence.

I also want to thank the wonderful spiritual community we affectionately call Christ Community Church. Thanks for giving me the privilege of sharing life together in Christ with you. May each day be lived as the last one, before our Audience of One!

FOREWORD BY JOE WHITE

Tom Nelson and David, King of Israel, make a great team. *Five Smooth Stones* is a true and unique reflection of the heart of the man who wrote it and the heart of the man about whom it is written. Tom Nelson and David are in every sense of the word "men after God's own heart." (After reading this fantastic book your own pilgrimage to the Cross will undoubtedly be more reflective of that same wonderful description!)

Tom and David also share a lion's heart for God. As David pounded Heaven's door with a quest to love God wholeheartedly and serve Him fervently, so does Tom. (I've observed him with admiration for over two decades.)

Again this book will draw that same quality out of you. *Five Smooth Stones* is also written to teach, train, instruct, and exhort. Men and women, we need our stones. We're lost in this crazy world of Satan's Goliaths without them. This book will fill your pocket with practical stones of wisdom so that you, too, can literally dance in front of the Goliaths that face you today and will face you in your future and say, ". . . but I come against you in the name of the Lord Almighty....this day the Lord will hand you over to me, and I'll strike you down.....all those gathered here will know that it is not by sword or spear that the Lord saves; for the battle is the Lord's." (1 Samuel 17)

Dr. Joe White, President
Kanakuk Kamps, Inc.

INTRODUCTION

Few memories from my childhood remain more embla-
zoned on my soul than those of the old rusty well handle that
imposingly stood out amid the polished granite remembrances
of my Scandinavian relatives. As a young boy growing up in the
tranquility of rural Minnesota, I found that even a visit to a near-
by cemetery was a welcomed interruption to my mundane of
farm life. As we bounced over gravel roads for the mile and a
half journey in our old jalopy, I was enveloped not only by chok-
ing dust, but also with great anticipation.

On special summer holidays, as well as when the summer
Minnesota rains failed to materialize, keeping the flowers thriv-
ing on our relatives' graves was essential. That meant water! "A
good dousing" as my mother described it. She always paid special attention to my father's grave. Something about new life
growing near his headstone eased the pain of death that the
grave so coldly proclaimed.

Rather than linger at my father's headstone trying to comprehend the incomprehensible, I set out for the old rusty, cast
iron well that stood as a timeless silhouette against the setting
summer sun. I wanted water—lots of water to fill the old dent-
ed bucket beneath the well handle. Expectantly, I placed the
bucket under the well's spout. I reached up, stretching my small
hands to their limit, grasping the cold cast iron. Then with all of
the force a six-year old could muster, I pulled the handle down.
Like the hideous screech of fingernails on a chalkboard, the col-
lision of rusting metal against rusty metal revolted me. But nothing was more devastating than the stunning realization that not
a drop of water was coming out of the well.

Undaunted, I summoned the courage to try again. I pulled

the pump handle down, enduring the hideous racket. And once again nothing!

At that moment of desperation my mother appeared beside me. Sensing my devastation, she quickly assured me that the well was not dry. With a smile she said, "Son, there's lots of water down there, but we need to do something first."

"What's that, Mom?" I asked.

She gently replied, "We need to prime the pump."

I watched as my mom picked up an old tattered coffee can, its distinguishing characteristics and advertising claims now shrouded by rust and a bullet hole. How the bullet hole got there, I wasn't sure. But I was convinced it proved rural Minnesota was anything but a dull place.

The water in that old coffee can saved the day. My mom poured that small amount of water into the top of the pump casing and said, "Ok, now pump the handle."

Once again I pulled the handle down. No water! Was this a joke? Or did my mom know something I didn't? She looked at me again and said, "Do it again son, pump the handle."

I pulled the handle and to my surprise, water began to gush out of that old pump. So much water flowed, in fact, that my bucket began to overflow. The more I pumped the well, the more gushers of water came out. I passionately pumped until my muscles ached. I had never before experienced such exhilaration.

I learned an important lesson that day from the old pump in the cemetery. You can't really experience the refreshment of a deep well unless you have a little water to prime the pump. In our quest for an authentic spirituality, I believe our experience is a lot like mine in that cemetery. With good intentions and with great sincerity we seek a meaningful spirituality—yet our souls are languishing, thirsty for living water. A haunting emptiness accompanies our journey. Though we expend effort, often, little if any water comes from the pump.

In my spiritual journey with Jesus Christ, I have been privileged to find living water that truly satisfies the deepest longings of the soul. Jesus promised his followers this would indeed be the case. Jesus said, "Whoever drinks of the water that I shall give him shall never thirst, but the water that I shall give him shall become in him a well of water springing up to eternal life" (John 4:14).

My heart's deep desire is to share with you some of the living water of grace and truth that I have found in Jesus. Any human work, however insightful and well intentioned, can only prime your pump. It will not completely satisfy your soul. No book can substitute your own prayerful study of the Holy Scriptures. My prayer is merely that these thoughts may whet your appetite for more.

Five Smooth Stones is designed to take you on an exhilarating journey through which you will investigate the most uncharted space in the universe—the unfathomable depths of the human soul. In this quest you will discover the path to authentic spirituality—a quest that demands discipline, grace, courage, and concentration, but one well worth the effort.

May the living water that I have found make your soul thirsty to plumb the depths of life in Jesus Christ. The well is deep and refreshing. I am just beginning to discover the wonder and majesty of it all. May you discover it too!

CONTENTS

1

Experiencing the Spiritual Birth

Jesus answered him, "I assure you, most solemnly I tell you, unless a person is born again, he cannot ever see the kingdom of God." John 3:3

Brian bolted out of his last class of the day with a burst of enthusiasm. Tonight was the big night—his first date with Amber, the prettiest girl in the school. He wanted the night to be absolutely perfect!

On his way home, Brian stopped by the mall to visit his favorite candy store. With passion exuding from every pore, Brian walked into the store and blurted out to the man behind the counter, "I want three boxes of candy, please—one large box, one medium sized box and a one small box."

The sales clerk was puzzled. He asked Brian, "I'm curious. Why do you want three different sized boxes of candy?"

Brian couldn't contain his excitement and explained, "I have a date tonight with the most popular girl in my class. Her name is Amber. If Amber lets me hold her hand, I'm going to give her a small box of candy. But if she lets me put my arm around her, I'll give her a medium sized box of candy."

"Wow," the man behind the counter said, "You've really thought this out. What's the large box of candy for?"

Brian said, "If I get to hold her hand, put my arm around her, *and* give her a good night kiss, I will give Amber this big box of candy." Brian picked up the three boxes of candy and headed home.

Later, all primped and proper, Brian arrived at Amber's house where her father greeted him at the door. Amber thought Brian seemed a bit nervous. First date jitters she reasoned.

After exchanging formal greetings, Amber's parents insisted that Brian stay for dinner. When they were seated at the dinner table, piled with mountains of scrumptious foods, Amber's father asked Brian to say grace. All those at the table bowed their heads and Brian began to pray. And Brian prayed, and he prayed, and he prayed some more! Not only was the food getting cold, but an even colder awkwardness filled the air as Brian kept praying. Finally, after what seemed like eternity and much to Amber's relief, Brian finished praying.

Thankfully, dinner was uneventful after that, and soon Brian and Amber headed out the door on their first date. As they got into Brian's car, Amber looked at Brian and blurted out, "Brian, I didn't know you were so religious."

Brian's face flushed bright red as he looked at Amber and said, "I didn't know your dad owned the candy store!"

I believe each of us has a lot of Brian in us. Like Brian we struggle to live a life of spiritual authenticity. Unfortunately, we often find ourselves living a "candy-store-Christianity," depicted by a nice looking religious facade, but contrasted by a vastly different inner self. In the shadows of our suffocating souls lurks the hideous monster of spiritual duplicity or deceit. Too often our Christianity is little more than a thin religious veneer wrapped around a thick secular core. Yet we find it much too easy to parrot the religious lines and still be vastly different inside.

Tragically, rather than becoming whole, we become very skillful at living a lie.

George and the Soviet Union

Our human capacity to live a lie was brought home to me in a compelling way when my wife and I spent several weeks with a group of American college students in what was then the Soviet Union. I will never forget when we crossed the Finnish border into the Soviet Union. Instantly, we encountered a brave new world tucked behind the iron curtain. Nothing could have prepared me for one of my most memorable life moments.

As American guests of the Soviet people, we received the red carpet treatment at many cultural exchange parties. We soon realized these cultural exchange parties had a very specific purpose—to promote the wondrous virtues of the Marxist/Leninist Soviet society. Each young idealistic Soviet I visited with echoed a very scripted party line. The lack of authenticity was beginning to make me feel nauseated—until I met George.

Like his counterparts, George first parroted the communist party line with utmost precision and flare, but as we talked more, he began to ask sincere questions about America. Towards the end of the evening, George told me he would like to visit more with me.

"Tom," he said, "I want to take you for a drive in my car tomorrow morning."

I was a bit surprised at first, skeptical of George's motives. As George persisted, I realized he wouldn't take no for an answer, so I reluctantly agreed.

Sure enough, George appeared early the next morning, eager to go. I had no idea where we were going, and uneasiness came over me as I hopped into his battered jalopy. In the car, we made small talk, and then George insisted that he wanted me to see his radio. I thought, "Radio! What's the big deal about a radio anyway?" Not wanting to reveal my true thoughts, I blurted out, "Yeah, George, that will be great!"

For the next hour and a half, we drove further and further into the recesses of the Caucus Mountains. With each switchback, the reaches of civilization moved further beyond our grasp. A tug of war erupted in my heart. On one hand my curiosity was reaching new heights, and on the other hand, my anxiety tugged at my chest. I shot up a couple of quick prayers.

Suddenly, George stopped the car. He looked at me and said, "My radio is up there!"

George pointed to a narrow path ascending into the thick, leafy woods. At that moment, everything seemed surreal. Was I dreaming? I thought, "Here I am in the middle of the Caucus Mountains with a Soviet guy named George whom I just met last night. No one in the world knows we are here. No one could find me, even if they wanted to."

Fighting my growing sense of fear, I got out of the car and followed George on the path. We walked for about a half-mile, continuing our ascent. My lungs gasped for breath and my head pounded. I was longing for a break when we suddenly reached a small clearing. George did not pause for a moment. He was so excited he was ready to burst.

Walking around an earth and shelter bunker on the side of the mountain, we came to a padlocked door. George pulled out a key from his prized Western patched blue jeans and opened the squeaky door. A musty smell teased my nostrils as I followed George into the bunker. Suddenly, with the flick of a switch, a low wattage bulb revealed George's well-concealed world. The room was filled with Western books, magazines and his prized possession—a ham radio that connected him to the outside world.

I couldn't contain my sense of shock. I looked at George and blurted out, "But George, what about all that stuff you said about the great Soviet society and the imperialistic, capitalistic West?"

George looked at me in amazement! "I don't believe all that! It's just the water we have to swim in. It's not the air that we breathe!"

My experience with George, and with others in the Soviet Union, made me see for the first time how easy it is for an entire population to live a lie. It was simple for them to parrot the party line, to learn the lingo, but to be vastly different on the inside. They learned to live a life of duplicity rather than one of integral wholeness!

And if we are truly honest, like my friend George, we can too easily swim in religious water—going through all the expected motions—but breathing a very different kind of air. Yet our hearts yearn passionately for authentic spirituality; our souls long for true wholeness. Deep inside we long for an integral, living, breathing faith.

In his book *A Place to Stand* Elton Trueblood reminds us that we must cultivate three areas if our spirituality is to be a whole, integral, living faith: The inner life of devotion, the intellectual life of rational thought, and the outer life of human service.[i] The path to true wholeness is both a feast for heart and mind and a journey that encounters true spiritual community with others.

The renewed interest in spiritual things and spirituality is a welcome development in our postmodern world. Yet this cultural quest into the non-material realm brings a great vulnerability to spiritual deception. Our society blindly accepts the deception that all "spiritualities" are on equal footing and that all roads lead to the same destination even if their claims to truth are contradictory.

From virtually every corner of culture, we're told all "spiritualities"—whether Buddhism, Christianity, or some avant-garde New Age spirituality—lead us to spiritual enlightenment and wholeness. Driving this trend is the strong cultural impulse for spiritual tolerance and compassionate pluralism.

Whether we are spiritual seekers lost in this confusing cultural maze or regular church-attenders immersed in a deadly and duplicitous candy-store-Christianity, the only way to find authentic spirituality is through a transforming encounter with Jesus Christ.

About Nicodemus

Nicodemus was a man who had an awakening of soul that forever changed his life. Nicodemus was a well-educated, well-connected, and well-respected spiritual leader of the Sanhedrin, the elite religious body of the day. According to chapters two and three in the Gospel of John, Nicodemus was intrigued by Jesus' wondrous works and teachings. Ultimately he decided to visit Jesus, although notably at night.

> *Now when He (Jesus) was in Jerusalem at the Passover, during the feast, many believed in His name observing His signs which He was doing. But Jesus, on His part, was not entrusting Himself to them, for He knew all men, and because He did not need anyone to testify concerning man, for He Himself knew what was in man. Now there was a man of the Pharisees, named Nicodemus, a ruler of the Jews; this man came to Jesus by night and said to Him, "Rabbi we know that you have come from God as a teach-*

er for no one can do these signs that you do unless God is with him." John 2:23-3:2

An Amazing Conversation

While Nicodemus was a well-intentioned and sincere religious man, he was an unenlightened man. He had not yet discovered the path to authentic spirituality. In an amazing conversation, Jesus showed him the way:

> *Jesus answered and said to him, "Truly, truly, I say to you, unless one is born again he cannot see the kingdom of God."*
>
> *Nicodemus said to Him, "How can a man be born when he is old? He cannot enter a second time into his mother's womb and be born can he?"*
>
> *Jesus answered, "Truly, truly, I say to you, unless one is born of water and the Spirit he cannot enter into the kingdom of God. That which is born of the flesh is flesh, and that which is born of the Spirit is spirit. Do not be amazed that I said to you, 'You must be born again.' The wind blows where it wishes and you hear the sound of it, but do not know where it comes from and where it is going, so is everyone who is born of the Spirit."*
>
> *Nicodemus answered and said to Him, "How can these things be." Jesus answered and said to him, "Are you the teacher of Israel and do not understand these things?" John 3:3-10*

In these eight verses, Jesus guided Nicodemus down the path of authentic spirituality. Jesus got right to the heart of the issue in verse three, "Jesus answered him, 'I assure you, most solemnly I tell you, unless a person is born again, he cannot ever see the kingdom of God.'"

To understand these verses, we must first remember this was a conversation between two religious and well-informed rabbis. Rabbis regularly gave authoritative pronouncements in matters of the law and spiritual matters, much as a judge would today. The repetition of "truly, truly" was a way to emphasize what Jesus was about to say. Jesus was not engaging in a theological speculation here; He was authoritatively teaching. We also must understand in this conversation, the words chosen by our Lord Jesus were filled with Old Testament connections.

The common ground of discussion in this passage is the kingdom of God, which is referred to in verse three, and repeated in verse five. The kingdom of God in its basic essence is the effective rule of God's sovereign will. Because God is personal and not a mere impersonal "force," such as in *Star Wars,* He has a domain or a kingdom that reflects His will. This kingdom is eternal in its dimensions and infinite in its scope. Jesus later stood before Pontius Pilate and said, "My kingdom is not of this world." By emphasizing "the kingdom of God" Jesus not only pointed the way to authentic spirituality, but emphasized that God is a personal Being.

"Truly, truly, I say to you, unless one is born again,[ii] he cannot see the kingdom of God," Jesus declared in verse three. He told Nicodemus that the path to authentic spirituality requires a spiritual birth. By employing the metaphor of a new birth, Jesus reminded Nicodemus that the human soul, sinful and separated from a Holy God, cannot be renovated by religious effort, but must be regenerated by God Himself. For the human soul to know God, that soul must first be infused with life from God. In the natural realm, we would consider anyone who claimed he had birthed himself as absolutely absurd.

One of my great joys as a pastor is going to the hospital after a baby is born. Recently a couple in our church, Sarah and Brian, had a baby boy named Miles. Soon after he was born, I had the pleasure of holding this little guy in my arms, and watching him peacefully sleep. We marveled together as patches of "Godlight" filled the hospital room. A sense of wonder filled our hearts as we gazed at this true masterpiece.

Sarah and Brian had obviously played a part in this masterpiece. Yet they were more like bystanders, mere instruments in God's creation of a new soul. Physical birth demands something outside of ourselves.

This is also true in the spiritual realm. This is why Jesus tells us that we cannot by our own effort or merit pull ourselves up to enter the kingdom of God through some religious renovation. No wonder Nicodemus was so astounded. During his whole life he had followed the Torah and the law—hoping to become good enough to be accepted by God. Jesus destroyed the bubble of Nicodemus' prideful religious presumption by telling Nicodemus he was spiritually blind and needed to be born from above. Jesus clearly told Nicodemus that he could not experience true spirituality through the sincere but misguided conduit of his own religious effort.

How often we, like Nicodemus, fall into this deception that we can find authentic spirituality by religious effort or human merit. The tenacious barnacles of pride not only attach themselves to human vice, but also to religious virtue.

After examining this text, Commentator Leon Morris concluded, "These solemn words forever exclude the possibility of salvation by human merit."[iii]

Nicodemus was clearly stunned by what he heard. His sincere theological world was shattered. His spiritual paradigm was blown out of the water.

Max Lucado insightfully captures this moment when he writes:

> No chitchat here. No idle talk. Straight to the point. Straight to the heart. Straight to the problem. Jesus knows the heart of the legalist is hard. You can't crack it with feathery accolades. You need a chisel. So Jesus hammers away: You can't help the blind by turning up the light, Nicodemus. You can't help the deaf by turning up the music, Nicodemus. You can't change the inside by decorating the outside, Nicodemus. You can't grow fruit without seed, Nicodemus. You must be born again … . The meeting between Jesus and Nicodemus was more than an encounter between two religious figures. It was a collision between two philosophies. Two opposing views of salvation. Nicodemus thought the person did the work; Jesus says God does the work. Nicodemus thought it was a tradeoff. Jesus says it is a gift. Nicodemus thought man's job was to earn it. Jesus says man's job is to accept it.[iv]

Nicodemus' whole life had been devoted to studying the Old Testament law and pursuing religious objectives. Yet Jesus was telling him that without a spiritual birth, he was spiritually blind and could not even see God's kingdom. Jesus clearly showed that sincere religious devotion and a vast knowledge of the Law was not enough for Nicodemus, or any person, to achieve spiritual merit or eternal life!

Nicodemus' question in verse four was not so much insincere as it was to fill the dead air of the moment. What do we say when we don't know what to say? We usually say something shallow, silly, or just plain stupid.

Hoping to rebuild Nicodemus' shattered religious world, Jesus anchored the need for spiritual birth in common Old

Testament theological ground. In verses five through nine, Jesus utilized the word *spirit* four times and used the word *wind* once.[v]

To Rabbi Nicodemus, an expert in the Torah, Jesus' usage of *spirit* and *wind* immediately connected his mind with the creation account in Genesis. "The earth was formless and void, and darkness was over the surface of the deep, and the 'spirit' [ruach] of God was moving over the surface of the waters" (Gen. 1:2). Jesus was pointing Nicodemus to the cause of creation: the Spirit of God.

Just as the earth was formless, void, and dark, the human soul is void and dark, enslaved to sin, and alienated from God because of sin. Like the initial creation, every human soul must be created anew by God's spirit. The human soul cannot be renovated by human effort or even religious sincerity, but must become a new creation. It must be born from above by God alone.

In John 3:7, Jesus told Nicodemus, "Do not be amazed that I said to you, 'You must be born again.'"

It was as if Jesus was saying, "This is what the Scriptures clearly teach, Nicodemus. Why haven't you seen it?" After all, as a student of the Torah, Nicodemus had read the words of the prophet Ezekiel who clearly spoke about a new birth from God.

Then I will sprinkle clean water on you, and you will be clean; I will cleanse you from all your filthiness and from all your idols. Moreover I will give you a new heart and put a new spirit within you; and I will remove the heart of stone from your flesh and give you a heart of flesh. I will put my Spirit within you and cause you to walk in My statutes, and you will be careful to observe my ordinances. Ezek. 36:25-27

Following this, in chapter 37, the prophet Ezekiel saw a vision of a valley filled with dried skeletons, which was a compelling picture of a religious, but spiritually dead, people. The Lord reminded Ezekiel that only by God's spirit can the human soul be given life.

Jesus' word choices reminded Nicodemus that this was not a new teaching; the Old Testament clearly revealed that every human soul must be given life by God Himself. To think we can achieve true spirituality through human merit is as absurd as dry and parched human skeletons coming to life on their own. True life must be initiated and sustained by the Spirit of God. The path to authentic spirituality begins with a spiritual birth.

Today, amid a resurgence of spiritual interest, we must not lose sight of what authentic spirituality really is.

What is Authentic Spirituality?

Jesus' amazing conversation with Nicodemus reminds us of a profound and compelling truth—authentic spirituality is not a matter of acting different and religious, but of entirely *being* different. Authentic spirituality is not self-directed religious renovation, but is Christ's gracious and merciful regeneration. Holiness, or "wholeness" is first and foremost a state of *being* entirely different.

Dallas Willard is a refreshing voice in the spiritual confusion of our world. "Spirituality is a matter of another reality," Willard writes. "It is absolutely indispensable to keep before us the fact that it (Spirituality) is not a 'commitment' and it is not a 'lifestyle,' even though a commitment and a life-style will come from it."[vi]

The apostle Paul, who experienced a spiritual birth on the

road to Damascus, also reminds us that authentic spirituality is about being a new creation. Writing to the Corinthian church, Paul declared, "Therefore, if anyone is in Christ, he is a new creation, the old has gone, the new has come!" (2 Cor. 5:17, NIV).

If Jesus Christ is the author of the new birth, then what is our responsibility? Jesus said those who enter the kingdom of God must be like children. Matthew 18:2-3 illustrates, "And He called a child to Himself and set him before them, and said, 'Truly, I say to you, unless you are converted and become like children, you will not enter the kingdom of heaven.'"

Jesus reminds each of us who desire authentic spirituality that we must become like children. Think for a moment about a child's heart. It is filled with wonder! It is filled with transparency! It is filled with sincerity! It is filled with dependency.

Bed Time Wars!

Trying to get our two young children to bed at night is often difficult. We call it "Bedtime Wars." Actually, my daughter Sarah, in particular, will try anything to delay going to bed. A last minute snack! A drink of water! And then, of course, we have her ritual good night hug for our dog Lady. But when I wait for her by the stairs, Sarah knows her well-devised diversions have been exhausted—along with my patience. The dreaded time has come to go upstairs and get ready for bed.

Just before she ascends the stairs, however, another special ritual occurs. Standing on the third step while I stand at the bottom of the stairs, she holds up her arms, and with her eyes closed she jumps into my arms. Then we hug all the way up the stairs. Though I am tired from the day, climbing the stairs seems effortless with my daughter in my arms. It is a cherished, fleeting moment. During this nightly ritual, I am repeatedly reminded the heart of a child holds complete trust when he or she knows someone loves him or her unconditionally.

A Crucial Response!

Likewise, when we come to Christ, we come to Him as children. Our hearts are filled with the wonder of Him! The Messiah, who left the throne of heaven, came to this earth, died on a cross for our sins, and was raised on the third day. The apostle Paul captures the reality of God's amazing love in sending Christ as our Savior from sin. "He [God the Father] made Him who knew no sin [God the Son] to be sin on our behalf that we might become the very righteousness of God in Him [God the Son]" (2 Cor. 5:21).

What good news! What an amazing swap! Our vile sin for Jesus' perfect righteousness is made available to all who will embrace Him in child-like faith and humble repentance. When we come to Christ as children, our hearts are transparent before Him. We become vulnerable and honest with Christ, admitting our sin and repenting from it. Our hearts are filled with dependency before Him. We place our complete trust in Him as our wonderful Savior and our majestic Lord.

Jesus described the heart reality of child-like wonder, transparency, humility and dependency as "believing faith." To trust Christ with believing faith is to believe that He is right about everything and that He is completely reliable.

Jesus reminds Nicodemus in verse 16, "For God so loved the world, that He gave His only begotten Son, that whoever believes in Him shall not perish, but have eternal life."

In the ultimate mystery of the universe, God's unfathomable love reaches down to us, through Christ, and infuses our soul with life. That's when our journey of authentic spirituality begins. We are transformed in Christ. We are transferred from the kingdom of darkness to the kingdom of light. Paul writes, "For He rescued us from the domain of darkness, and transferred us to the kingdom of His beloved Son" (Col. 1:13). When we are born from above, we enter an entirely new reality—one that we could not even see or fathom in our spiritual blindness.

A Lesson from Pascal

One of the most influential minds and a powerful spiritual presence in the seventeenth century church was the French physicist, philosopher and theologian, Blaise Pascal. When he died, those preparing his body for burial found sewn into Pascal's clothing a piece of parchment he carried with him at all times:

> The year of grace 1654, Monday 23, November . . . from about half past ten in the evening until half past midnight. Fire! 'God of Abraham, God of Isaac, God of Jacob, not of philosophers and scholars. Certainty, certainty, heartfelt, joy, peace. God of Jesus Christ. God of Jesus Christ. My God and your God. Thy God shall be my God. The world forgotten, and everything except God. He can only be found by the ways taught in the Gospels. Greatness of human soul. O righteous Father, the world has not known thee, but I have known thee. Joy, joy, joy, tears of joy.[vii]

The deepest longings of Pascal's searching soul were met in Jesus Christ. Oh the life-changing reality of spiritual birth!

In our quest to find authentic spirituality, a true wholeness of soul, we must not miss this foundational truth taught by our Lord Jesus Christ. The most important question all of us must ask ourselves is this: "Have I been born again?"

Have You Been Born Again?

People often ask me, "Tom, how do I know if I have truly experienced a spiritual birth?" When you're born again, you won't necessarily see the clouds part and hear the angels sing. For some, spiritual birth is as dramatic as the apostle Paul's experience on the road to Damascus, when he suddenly encountered God's voice. But for many, spiritual birth is a quiet, yet life-changing moment with Christ.

Jesus said spiritual birth is like the wind—you cannot immediately see it, but the effects of its presence cannot be hidden. When you embrace Jesus Christ as your Lord and Savior, the desires of your heart and the longings of your soul begin to change. The fruit of God's spirit (love, joy, peace, patience, kindness, goodness, faithfulness, gentleness, self-control) begin to germinate in the spiritually fertile soil of your soul. You begin to experience life as God intended. A soul without true spiritual life in Christ is like eating when you have a cold—all is tasteless and hauntingly unfulfilling.

Nicodemus was a sincere, religious man. He knew about spiritual things. He was even a fixture at the synagogue. Yet he was far from the kingdom of God—until he met Jesus. Scripture tells us Nicodemus' life changed. He became a follower of Jesus. He found wholeness of soul in Jesus Christ. His heart's cries for love, meaning, and significance were answered.

In the spiritual confusion of our postmodern world and the superficial candy store-type Christianity so often found in the church, we must not forget that right decisions, rather than sincere desire, determine our destiny. Through the keyhole of our finite reason and the created world around us, we get a passing, blurred glimpse of spiritual reality. But Jesus the Messiah holds the key that unlocks the door to seeing the kingdom of God. The path to authentic spirituality, to wholeness of soul, begins by being born again in Jesus Christ.

Closing Thoughts

The great New England poet, Robert Frost, captured in one of his best-loved poems, *The Road Not Taken,* the significance of our choices at defining moments in our fleeting earthly lives. Sometimes, *The Road Less Traveled* makes all the difference.

Jesus said, "Enter through the narrow gate, for the gate is wide and the way is broad that leads to destruction, and many are those who enter through it. For the gate is small and the way is narrow that leads to life, and there are few that find it" (Matt. 7:13-14).

The path to authentic spirituality is not a wide road, but a narrow one—a path that begins with a spiritual birth. It is the road less traveled!

Questions

In what ways do you find yourself living a "Candy Store Christianity?" *Not wanting to short change myself. Yet wanting praise from my friends. Not wanting to be embarrassed in front of other Christians.*

Tom quotes his Russian friend, George, as saying, "I don't believe all that. It's just the water we have to swim in; it's not the air we breathe." How might George's comments reflect your spiritual journey? *George was trying to keep a correct focus on God in a difficult situation. He would do best to do the same. We or God are hiding his light.*

Comment on Tom's assessment of contemporary Christianity. Do you agree? Disagree? Why?

yes, people do not want to face the truth that Jesus is the only way to the Father - Satan has deceived them.

What do you think was Jesus' main point in His encounter with Nicodemus in John 3?

That you must be born again by the Spirit of God!

How do Jesus' words to Nicodemus ring true for us today?

Each one of us must be Born again of the Holy Spirit

Why is a spiritual birth necessary to experience the kingdom of God? *Because our sin separates us from God & our Spiritual rebirth cleanses us so that we may be w/ Him.*

Comment on Tom's assertion, "Authentic spirituality is not different religious action, but entirely different being." How might 2 Corinthians 5:17 buttress this assertion?

Because when we are made new the old passes away & we start over anew, w/o blemish.

Share about your spiritual birth experience.

young girl, 7 or 8, knew ___ w

2

Putting On Jesus' Easy Yoke

Take My yoke upon you and learn of Me, for I am gentle and humble in heart, and you will find rest for your souls. Matthew 11:29

Oksano Bauyo was the winner of the women's figure skating gold medal in the 1994 winter Olympic games in Lillehammer, Norway. With a stunning performance of athletic perfection, this sixteen-year-old girl from Russia edged out the favored American skater, Nancy Kerrigan, and skated to the top of the world. Fame and fortune arrived, but true fulfillment did not!

Driving her new $100,000 Mercedes, Oksano crashed into a tree and was arrested for drunken driving. Like her shiny car, Oksano's life was spinning out of control, heading for a devastating crash.

On a *48 Hours* television special highlighting the winter Olympic games in Nagano, Japan, Oksano was interviewed by Susan Spencer. Behind a video collage of her spectacular athletic achievements, we heard whimpers of a languishing soul. Oksano talked about her tragic fall from skating grace, fueled by her alcohol abuse. Susan Spencer looked Oksano directly in the eyes and with compassionate incredulity asked her, "Why did you drink?"

Without batting an eyelash, Oksano candidly replied, "To feel good about myself."[i]

As I was drawn into this compelling interview, I was deeply moved by recognizing a reality we are often reluctant to admit: The deepest longings of our soul—our longing for love, meaning, significance, security, contentment, fulfillment, beauty, and wonder—are not found in the fame or fortune of this world.

Like mirages in a desert, fame and fortune beckon our parched souls. Deceptive images of power, prestige, prosperity and pleasure entice us. With reckless abandonment we chase them across desert dunes of time, only to see the empty, meaningless visions dissipate before our eyes.

In the mirror of Oksano Bauyo's languishing soul, we see a haunting shadow of our own souls. Listening to the cries of her heart, we hear the quiet whimpering of our own hearts.

In his book *The Call*, Os Guinness echoed the cries of our hearts when he observed, "The trouble is that as modern people we have too much to live with and too little to live for ... . in the midst of material plenty we have spiritual poverty."[ii]

Doug Webster author of *The Easy Yoke*, also observed the emptiness of our lives: "A strange paradox afflicts modern life. On the one hand, we have never had it so good; on the other, we have never been so empty ... . It is the best of times for recreation, the worst of times for righteousness. It is the best of times for healthcare, the worst of times for wholeness. It is the best of times for technology, the worst of times for truth."[iii]

Where is our emptiness filled? How are the deepest longings of our souls satisfied? Where is wholeness of soul found?

The Path to Wholeness of Soul

I believe the answer is found in what A.W. Tozer first described as "the rediscovery of a bedridden truth." Tozer wrote, "Bedridden truths are those often familiar words that lose all power of truth and lie bedridden in the dormitory of our languishing souls."

One bedridden truth that has transformed my spiritual journey is found in Christ's words:

> *At that time Jesus said, "I praise you, Father, Lord of heaven and earth, that you have hidden these things from the wise and the intelligent and have revealed them to infants. Yes, Father, for this way was well pleasing in your sight. All things have been handed over to Me by My father and no one knows the Son except the Father; nor does anyone know the Father, except the Son, and anyone to whom the Son wills to reveal Him."*
>
> *Come to Me, all who are weary and heavy-laden and I will give you rest. Take my yoke upon you and learn from Me, for I am gentle and humble in heart, and you shall find rest for your souls. For My yoke is easy and My burden is light." Matt. 11:25-30*

In these verses, Jesus gave us what I like to call "The Great Invitation." Danish philosopher and devout Christian Soren Kierkegaard captures the significance I place on this bedridden truth. "The thing is to understand myself to see what God really wants me to do, the thing is to find a truth which is true for me, to find the idea for which I can live and die," Kierkegaard wrote in his journal. The Great Invitation is just such a truth!

In examining The Great Invitation, let's look at three foundational questions:

Who is Jesus?

What does Jesus invite us to do?

What does Jesus promise to those who are yoked with Him?

Who is Jesus?

In a moment of praise to the Father, Jesus reiterates the truth that authentic spirituality demands our souls be infused with life from above in spiritual birth. Reason and intelligence alone will not transform the human soul. Religious works cannot do it. Self-renovation or sincere reformation will not bring spiritual birth. We must come to God with the heart of a child and be born again.

Like a light bulb, the human soul—no matter how hard it tries or how well its intents—cannot experience true light alone. It must have an energy source beyond itself.

In Matthew 11:27, as a member of the Triune Godhead, Jesus emphasized His absolute deity, power and authority. Notice in verse 27 Jesus declared that only through Him can the human soul know God. "All things have been handed over to Me by My Father; and no one knows the Son except the Father, nor does anyone know the Father, except the Son and anyone to whom the Son wills to reveal Him."

Jesus didn't stutter. He was absolutely clear. In verse 27, Jesus repeated the word "know" twice. This word suggests not merely a person's general cognitive knowledge, but an intimate relationship.

Jesus did not claim to be some mere prophet or spiritual

guru. He claimed to be God. He claimed to be the only way to God. In John 14:6, Jesus said, "I am the way, the truth and the life no one comes to the Father but by Me."

Jesus' disciples got the message. In Acts 4:12, Peter told all of Jerusalem, "And there is salvation in no one else, for there is no other name under heaven that has been given among men by which we must be saved."

How we answer the question, "Who is Jesus?" will determine the direction of our spiritual journey and our spiritual destiny.

In Faith's Hotseat

The large university lecture hall was packed with students dutifully taking notes. Day after day, the professor droned on about the development of Western civilization, carefully inserting ideological barbs designed to leave a lasting mark on impressionable minds and hearts.

Finally, he reached the subject of political/religious movements in the first century. As a follower of Christ, I sat in my chair, eager to hear what he would say about Jesus. I was sure he could not avoid talking about Jesus, but I was not prepared for what he would say. In a vitriolic manner, this professor blatantly abandoned any historical objectivity and created a very negative caricature of Jesus. He assaulted the historicity of the New Testament writers and attacked everything I believed.

As I continued to listen to this professor paint such a negative picture of Jesus and his followers, my heart pounded, my stomach did flip-flops and my armpits began to drip. I squirmed in my seat.

When the professor called Jesus a deluded joker, I couldn't stand it any more. Amid a sea of stunned students, I raised my hand. Silence blanketed the lecture hall as the professor saw my hand. Irritated at my interruption, he abruptly asked if I had a question. I am not exactly sure what I said; I only know time seemed to be suspended. I blurted something like, "Sir, I don't think it is fair or historically objective to characterize Jesus of Nazareth as a deluded joker when his life and teaching have so profoundly shaped and continue to shape Western civilization."

The professor responded with those dreaded words. "I want to see you in my office after class." I don't think I heard a word of the rest of his lecture. I could only think about the serious trouble I was in with this guy.

After the class was finally over, I walked to his office. I felt like I was on the death row march. I mustered the courage to knock on his door. He told me to come in, to shut the door, and to sit down. As I sat, my heart began to race all over again. My professor asked my name and said, "You must be a follower of Jesus."

"Yes, I am," I squeaked.

There I was perched, on the hotseat of faith, bracing myself for a verbal barrage of ridicule, but his next words shocked me. To my amazement, this professor shared how he had studied in a Christian seminary and had been ordained, but had become disillusioned with all he had seen and experienced. So to make some sense of his shattered world, he pursued the path of University academia.

As he talked, my emotions evolved from fear to compassion for a man with a sharp intellect, but with an embittered heart. This was a man who had experienced the tyranny of religion and had tragically missed an intimate relationship with Jesus!

After that day, we never talked about Jesus again.

Thankfully, I passed the class, but I was reminded how Jesus' claims and teachings are a stumbling block to many and often go against the grain of our politically correct culture.

Jesus' words are exclusive, and at times, from our finite vantage point, they do seem intolerant. But Jesus' Messianic mission was to declare the truth to the world—His goal was not just to win friends and influence people. Jesus did not come to tickle our ears, but to transform our hearts. The Messiah did not merely enter our world to enhance our self-esteem, but to invade our souls with life from above.

In our obsession to be perceived as tolerant, we seldom stop and ask what is intolerable to God. The ultimate intolerance is to distort God's clearly revealed truth. If we are to discover the path to authentic spirituality, we must understand who Jesus really is. A faulty view of Jesus will inevitably lead to a faulty spirituality. Certainly, the many cults and toxic faith environments testify to this perverse malady of our society.

The Jesus of Holy Scripture is the eternal Son of God, fully God, Co-creator of the universe. Jesus is the Son of God who left heaven and became a man; the Messiah who was born in Bethlehem, died on a Roman cross for our sins, was raised from the dead on the third day, ascended into Heaven, and will one day return as the conquering King. He is the Lamb who was slain—the judge of all—and is worthy to be worshiped. Every knee will bow before Him. He is the alpha and the omega. Out of the unfathomable depths of His love, this Jesus extends to you and me the greatest invitation ever given.

What Does Jesus Invite Us to Do?

My wife, Liz, and I have received many invitations in the

mail over the years, but one stands above the rest. When it arrived in our mailbox, we rushed to open it. This invitation was from the White House, boldly stamped with the gold lettering of the official Presidential Seal. Our hearts skipped a beat. This was the President's invitation to a banquet in Washington D.C. for celebrating the Year of the Bible.

When we received the invitation, we looked at our busy schedule and thought, "Oh, we don't have time for this," right? Wrong! Like a piece of junk mail we tossed it into the trash, right? Wrong!

No, this invitation was different! Why? Because of who sent it. Our eyes were set on Washington D.C. and we weren't about to let anything deter us.

In Matthew 11:28-30, Jesus Christ, the Prince of Peace—not just the President, but the Creator of the whole world, not just the leader of the free world—offers each of us a great invitation. But, so often we go "ho-hum." As if we've received a piece of junk mail, we toss it into the trash. Yet Jesus' great invitation is anything but boring. It is an invitation to experience life as God intended—to fellowship with the triune God for all eternity. We are given an invitation to experience intimacy with God Himself.

In this scripture we are called to a sacred romance with the greatest lover of our soul. We are not given merely a road map to success, but a life compass setting for true significance. Jesus calls each of us not primarily to do great things, but to become an apprentice of a great Person. Jesus desires our intimacy with Him much more than our accomplishment for Him.

What does Jesus invite us to do? Jesus invites us to come to Himself, the King of kings, the Master of masters, and enter into an intimate apprenticeship. Jesus invites us to enter into His yoke. Because of our technological advancement, we are not very familiar with the yoke, but the yoke was common in an agrarian culture. As a young boy, Jesus worked in a carpenter's shop and probably learned how to make yokes for farmers. What is the significance of Jesus using the metaphor of the yoke?

Jesus Invites Us To Be Yoked With Him

The yoke was a common tool used as oxen plowed the fields. It was like a McDonald's® golden arches turned upside down with a large wooden beam over the top. In Jesus' day, each yoke was custom made by a skilled carpenter for a specific team of oxen.

The farmer would put two oxen in the yoke side by side. He would put the mature, experienced ox on the larger side of the yoke and the younger, inexperienced ox on the other side. In the yoke, the young ox became an apprentice to the experienced ox. The young ox, used to unbridled selfish pursuits, would want to go off the path when he saw green grass. The mature ox would pull him back and keep him on course. When the young ox entered the yoke, he left an old way of life and submitted to a new master that would train him. The young ox would get to intimately know the other ox and learn everything the older one knew. In the course of time, the young ox would become like the mature ox.

The yoke is the picture Jesus paints for those of us who want to be his true disciples, his authentic followers. The yoke was often a symbol of enslavement and oppression, but Jesus used it as a symbol of ultimate freedom.

Today, we cannot escape the symbol of the cross, but what happened to the symbol of the yoke? What happened to the yoke of Christ? Does this give us some hints about the status of contemporary Christianity and the anemic state of the church of Jesus Christ?

"We have made following Jesus easy in the convenient, casual sense of the word…instead of a yoke, we have been given a free pass to the next performance. Instead of sojourners, we are spectators," Doug Webster writes. "Instead of the body of Christ, we are a religious audience. Yet without the yoke, life is unbearable."[iv]

Why has Christ's yoke become a bedridden truth today? Perhaps it is because we are self-absorbed. To undertake Christ's yoke demands total self-abandonment, which opposes our narcissistic behavior.

Dietrich Bonhoeffer, a courageous German pastor who stood up to the tyranny of Hitler and eventually paid for this with his life, wrote these timeless words, "When Christ calls a man, He bids him come and die."[v]

Jesus' words in John 12:24 echo this foundational truth, "Truly, truly, I say to you, unless a grain of wheat falls to the earth and dies, it remains alone; but if it dies, it bears much fruit."

In Mark, Jesus declares, "If anyone wishes to come after Me, he must deny himself and take up his cross and follow Me. For whoever wishes to save his life will lose it, but whoever loses his life for My sake and the gospel's will save it. For what does it profit a man to gain the whole world, and forfeit his soul?"

In a day when "disciple" is often thrown around and diluted of it's meaning, we must understand what Jesus means when he extends to us His great invitation.

The true disciple follows Jesus' lead and learns from Him just as an apprentice learns from a master craftsman, or as a resident doctor learns from an established physician.

The true disciple not only embraces Jesus' precepts, but also his practices. As a disciple, I have entered a self-abandoned, intimate apprenticeship with Jesus and am learning to live as He would live if He were me.

Putting on the yoke of Jesus changes our lives and our view of the world. We begin to grasp the realization of Christ's eternal kingdom. His yoke alters our values and priorities. As Doug Webster writes, "Being a disciple of Jesus is not a hobby. We are not disciples the way we are members of the Sierra Club or Rotary. One does not take up the easy yoke the way one takes up golf. The Christian life becomes an impossible burden when it is lived part-time or approached halfheartedly. Following Jesus requires everything else in life to be integrated with our commitment to Christ."[vi]

Jesus' Promise To Those Who Are Yoked With Him

In Jesus' yoke we learn to live as God intended for us to live. In the yoke of Christ, our hearts' deepest longings are met. In His yoke—and only in his yoke—our soul experiences wholeness.

Jesus gives an awesome promise in Matthew 11:29. Those who enter Jesus' yoke of discipleship "will find rest for their souls." The word rest often indicated passivity or relief from pressures and burdens of life. But this is not what Jesus meant. Rest is experiencing life as God intended. Rest is finding true fulfillment and wholeness of soul. This is what St. Augustine had in mind when he said, "Oh Lord, our souls are restless until they find their rest in You."

In verse 30 Jesus describes his yoke as easy. Easy does not mean devoid of effort, but "that which fits us perfectly." Jesus' yoke is custom-made for us. It fits us and lets us live as God intended for us to live. In Christ's yoke, we stand eyeball to eyeball with the Master. In this yoke, our hearts' affections change and Jesus recalibrates the setting of our life compass. Jesus' yoke is not a mirage in the desert, but is a well of living water that floods our souls with life-giving refreshment.

Without Jesus' yoke, we experience desperation of the soul. Much has been written about how the music of the Beatles in the 1960s reshaped the landscape of our culture. Of all the lyrics John Lennon wrote, the song *Help* I believe captures most his own desperation of soul.

When we cry "Help!" Jesus says, "Come to Me all you who are weary and heavy laden and I will give you rest. Take my yoke upon you and learn from me for I am gentle and humble of heart and you will find rest for your souls."

In reflection on the longings of our souls, C.S. Lewis said, "We are half-hearted creatures, fooling about with drink and sex and ambition, when infinite joy is offered us. Like an ignorant child who wants to go on making mud pies in a slum because he cannot imagine what is meant by the offer of a holiday at sea, we are far too easily pleased."[vii]

Jesus extends to us the greatest invitation imaginable. An invitation to be yoked with Him, to learn from Him, to become like Him, and to experience true wholeness of soul in Him. But being yoked with Jesus demands that we move from self-preoccupation to self-abandoned apprenticeship with Jesus. Christ's yoke demands surrender.

Are You Yoked With Jesus Christ?

G.K Chesterton gets to the bottom line of the matter when he states, "The problem with Christianity is not that it has been tried and found wanting, but that it has been found difficult and left untried."

What keeps us from responding to Jesus' invitation? Pride? Enslavement to pleasure, material possessions, or power? Peer pressure? Are we simply unwilling to rock the boat of our personal comfort?

Maybe our thirsty souls are chasing mirages, and we're deceiving ourselves that a self-absorbed life can bring true fulfillment. If so, we're feeding our empty souls on the garbage scraps of this world, rather than feasting at the scrumptious table of Christ. Those who put on the yoke of Christ are asked to lose their lives, but in that process they actually find their lives!

Learning To Soar!

One joy of adulthood is taking our children to the places where we grew up. As a youngster in Minnesota, I spent a lot of time fishing in a pristine river that ran lazily on the outskirts of my hometown. During one recent family vacation to Minnesota, my children and I decided to hike to a great spot where I had fished many times as a kid. The day was bright and sunny with puffy white cumulus clouds casting a periodic, passing shadow on the path. The cool air was invigorating. We sloshed along, the stubborn dew that had clung tenaciously to the grass now drenched our soggy feet. Yet we hardly even noticed—we were engrossed in the utopian optimism of a perfect fishing day in which we'd catch "the big one."

Arriving at my favorite fishing hole, we quickly baited our hooks and cast them into the water. In a matter of seconds, the red and white bobber attached to my son's line plunged underwater, his rod bending into a graceful arc. He had hooked a fish!

Then his sister's bobber also plunged. The fishing day was already living up to our expectations.

I don't know what distracted my attention from fishing. All of a sudden, to my right I saw a large bald eagle swoop right over the small dam where we were fishing. It was as if the eagle was doing touch and go landings on an aircraft carrier. I had never seen such precision and grace. For a moment I was breathless! Then I yelled, "Schaeffer! Sarah! Look! Look at the eagle!"

"Yeah, dad! That's pretty cool," Schaeffer replied and kept fishing. He didn't seem to comprehend this wasn't just an everyday occurrence in Minnesota. As quickly as the eagle had made its unannounced visit, it departed, flying effortlessly over the trees along the riverbank.

Although my children were focused on fishing, I marveled at seeing a bald eagle so close. Fishing didn't seem quite as exciting for me after that point. I began to scan the sky, searching for another glimpse of this majestic bird of prey.

I was rewarded by another sighting of the eagle. Only this time it flew considerably higher, its strong wings propelling it even higher into the atmosphere. Suddenly, the eagle stopped flying! It locked its massive wings and began to soar. Effortlessly, the bird of prey climbed higher and higher, its mighty wings capturing the power of the atmospheric thermo currents thousands of feet above.

I was mesmerized by the beauty of the moment. I have never before seen magnificent soaring on this level. Then it hit me! This eagle was created not only to fly with the strength of its strong wings, but to soar on currents far more powerful. But to soar, the eagle had to quit relying on its own strength, and rest on something much greater than itself. To soar, the eagle had to submit to the atmospheric thermo currents!

Like this eagle, we were created not only to fly, but to soar high on the currents of Jesus' grace and truth. How tragic that so few souls ever learn the secret of soaring. For soaring demands complete submission!

Those of us who want to embark the path to authentic spirituality must wear the easy yoke of Christ—a yoke that demands complete surrender. No shortcuts exist to soaring! Our decisions, not our desires, determine our destiny.

> *"Lord Jesus, teach me to soar high on the currents of your grace and truth. Grant me the faith and the courage to completely surrender. Refresh my longing soul with the invigorating breezes of eternity. Amen!"*

Questions

Why does Tom believe that Jesus' teaching in Matthew 11:28-30 is what A.W. Tozer described as a "bedridden truth?"

Because we hear it so often it becomes familiar ?

Tom asserts that the compelling significance of "The Great Invitation" is based on who extends it to us. Do you agree? Disagree? Why? *yes,*

How do you think a faulty view of Jesus will affect a person's spirituality? *you must really know who He is + what He says to withstand the storms of life*

In The Great Invitation, we find that our calling is not

primarily to do great things for God, but to become an apprentice of a great Person—Jesus Christ. Why is this such an important life-compass setting? *Because we must become more like Jesus - Be like Jesus*

Tom describes the training regimen of the newly yoked ox. How does your journey with Christ reflect the challenges and joys of the ox? *So many things distract yet you look at Christ & you see where you need to be & that brings great joy.*

Why is it so important that we not only embrace Jesus' precepts, but also His practices? *You must walk the talk*

What does Jesus promise to those who are His yoked apprentices? What does Jesus mean by "rest?" *True wholeness of soul*

What does it mean that Jesus' yoke is easy? What is the significance that Jesus' yoke is custom fit for you? *The yoke he has for us fits perfectly*

What does the yoke of Christ demand from us? Have you entered Jesus' yoke? *total surrender*

yes!

3

Shedding Saul's Armor

*Let us strip off and throw aside every encumbrance and
that sin which so readily clings to and entangles us, and let
us run with patient endurance and steady and active per-
sistence the appointed course of the race that is set before us.
Hebrews 12:1*

In his book, *A View From The Zoo,* former zookeeper Gary
Richmond describes his terrifying encounter with Ivan.

"I'll never forget the feelings I experienced when two shiny
new keys were pressed firmly into my trembling hands," wrote
Gary. "They weren't just any keys. These keys gave me access to
all the cages at the Los Angeles Zoo."

As the supervisor handed Richmond the keys, he reminded
the young man that the keys would let him in to care for mil-
lions of dollars worth of animals—some of them irreplaceable.
And if the animals got out, they might not only hurt themselves,
but someone else.

"You wouldn't want that on your conscience," the crusty old
veteran reminded Richmond.

Richmond also learned from his supervisor the value of a
consistent routine. So every day, Richmond followed exactly the

same procedures in caring for the animals. As a result, he received sterling evaluations for safety habits and performed flawlessly for four months. Then something happened.

"I couldn't tell you why my routine varied, but somehow it did and with the most dangerous animal at the zoo," Richmond recalls. "Ivan was a polar bear who weighed well over nine hundred pounds and had killed two prospective mates. He hated people and never missed an opportunity to attempt to grab anyone passing by his cage. Many of us had experienced nightmares featuring Ivan. And one of the thoughts most discussed among the keepers was the horrifying question, 'What if Ivan got out?'

"For more than one hundred consecutive workdays I had cared for this nightmare, never coming close to making a mistake. Then I let him out of his night quarters into the sparkling morning sunshine by pulling a lever that lifted a five-hundred-pound steel guillotine door. No sooner had he passed under it than I realized that I had left the steel door that had given me access to the outside exhibit—where he now was—wide open.

"At any minute he might be walking down the hall and around the corner. My inclination was to run. Not wanting to be fired, I chose to stay. I lifted the guillotine door again, and to my relief Ivan was in view. He was a creature of routine, and he always spent the first hour of his morning pacing. His pattern was L-shaped. He would walk from the door five steps straight out and then turn right for three steps. He would then rock back and forth and come back to the guillotine door, which he would bump up with his head. He would repeat that cycle for one hour and then rest.

"I timed his pacing cycle and determined that I had seventeen seconds to run down the hallway and shut the open door. I staked my life on his consistency. He didn't seem to notice the wide-open door, which was unusual. Animals tend to notice any change in their environment. I decided that when he made his next turn, I would run down the L-shaped concrete hallway, hoping upon hope that I would not see Ivan.

"He turned and I ran. With every step my knees weakened. My heart pounded so hard I felt sure it would burst from fear. I made the corner and faced the critical moment. Ivan was still out of sight; I lunged for the door handle. As I reached out for the handle, I looked to the right. There was the bear, eight feet away. Our eyes met. His were cold and unfeeling, and I'm sure mine expressed all the terror that filled the moment. I pulled the huge steel door with all my strength. It clanged shut and the clasp was secured.... I looked up, and Ivan was staring at me through the viewing window of the hallway door. I had almost let out a bear—the worst bear at the zoo."[i]

Though we may not have come eyeball-to-eyeball with a polar bear like Ivan, each of us faces giants in our lives—towers of terror that intimidate and paralyze us, stretching our souls on a frozen rope of fear.

Some of us face a giant in the form of the paralyzing fear of being rejected by friends at school or at work—a fear that keeps our faith locked in a cowardly closet and leads us to live dishonest Christian lives.

Maybe the tower of terror wreaking havoc in your journey with Christ is the fear of the unknown. Maybe you fear that if you give your life fully to Christ, it will mean a life of destitution and drudgery. Perhaps you fear this will mean living in a mud hut in some remote corner of the globe with a diet of insects and monkey brains?

For some of us, the giant is a deep fear of personal inadequacy. We cower in the corner of comfortability rather than venturing into an invigorating and vibrant faith. Perhaps the fear of failure imprisons our dreams behind bars of disobedience and unbelief.

Like us, God's people of old faced intimidating giants.

One of those giants was a literal 9-foot, 9-inch tower of terror who would make Rambo look like Pee Wee Herman. For forty days this recurring nightmare taunted God's people. With a winner-take-all wager, this giant held the Israelites at bay, frozen on the rope of fear. The biggest, brightest, and bravest of God's people cowered before him. That is, they cowered until a young shepherd boy named David arrived on the scene.

David and Goliath

In the familiar Bible story of David and Goliath (1 Samuel 17), we are reminded that those who pursue authentic spirituality must learn how to conquer the giants that loom in the soul:

> *As he was talking with them, behold the champion, the Philistine from Gath Goliath was coming up from the army of the Philistines, and he spoke these same words; and David heard them. When all the men of Israel saw the man, they fled from him and were greatly afraid. And the men of Israel said, "Have you seen this man who is coming up? Surely he is coming up to defy Israel. And it will be that the king will enrich the man who kills him with great riches and will give him his daughter and make his father's house free in Israel."*
>
> *Then David spoke to the men who were standing by him, saying, "What will be done for the man who kills this Philistine, and takes away the reproach of Israel? For who*

is this uncircumcised Philistine, that he should taunt the armies of the living God?" And the people answered him in accord with this word saying, " Thus it will be done for the man that kills him."

Now Eliab his oldest brother heard when he spoke to the men; and Eliab's anger burned against David and he said, "Why have you come down? And with whom have you left those few sheep in the wilderness? I know your insolence and the wickedness of your heart; for you have come down in order to see the battle." But David said, "What have I done now? Was it not just a question?" Then he turned away from him to another and said the same thing; and the people answered as before. When the words which David spoke were heard, they told them to Saul, and he sent for him. And David said to Saul, "Let no man's heart fail on account of him; your servant will go and fight with this Philistine." Then Saul said to David, "You are not able to go against this Philistine to fight with him; for you are but a youth while he has been a warrior from his youth." But David said to Saul, "Your servant was tending his father's sheep. When a lion or a bear came and took a lamb from the flock, I went out after him and attacked him and rescued it from his mouth; and when he rose up against me, I seized him by his beard and struck him and killed him. Your servant has killed both the lion and the bear and this uncircumcised Philistine will be like one of them, since he has taunted the armies of the living God." And David said," The Lord who delivered me from the paw of the lion and from the paw of the bear, he will deliver me from the hand *of this Philistine." And Saul said to David, "Go and may the Lord be with you."*

Then Saul clothed David with his garments and put a bronze helmet on his head, and he clothed him with armor. And David girded his sword over his armor and tried to walk, for he had not tested them. So David said to Saul, "I cannot go with these, for I have not tested them." And David took them off. 1 Samuel 17:23-39

Extracting A Profound Spiritual Truth

We must understand that David's remarkable victory over Goliath is not primarily a story about the extraordinary courage of a young shepherd boy who triumphs against all odds. Rather, this scripture is about David's extraordinary insight into spiritual battle.

In verses 26 and 36, David referred to the armies of the living God. What did he mean? While the armies of Israel were looking at the physical realm and cowering in fear, David saw the spiritual realm and was invigorated by faith. The others could only see an imposing giant. David saw Almighty God. Young David had great spiritual vision. That spiritual vision was apparent as he approached Goliath:

Then David said to the Philistine, "You come to me with a sword, a spear, and a javelin, but I come to you in the name of the Lord of hosts, the God of the armies of Israel whom you have taunted. This day the Lord will deliver you up into my hands, and I will strike you down and remove your head from you. And I will give the dead bodies of the

*armies of the Philistines this day to the birds of the sky and
the wild beasts of the earth, that all the earth may know
that there is a God in Israel, and that all this assembly may
know that the Lord does not deliver by sword or by spear,
for the battle is the Lord's and He will give you into our
hands." 1 Samuel 17:45-47*

David understood what we often forget: Spiritual battles cannot be won by human weapons. Giants of the soul cannot be
conquered with mere human wisdom or strength.

Before David approached the giant, he did something profound that we often overlook in this familiar story.

Saul, the King of Israel, was absolutely desperate to get rid of
Goliath. In giving David permission to take on Goliath, Saul
waged the whole battle, and the freedom of his own people, on
young David. Well-intentioned, King Saul put David in an awk-
ward situation; he offered the young boy his armor and
weapons.

David could not immediately refuse the king. So trying to
help David battle this giant, Saul smothered David with his own
armor. The sight must have been a bit humorous. David could
hardly walk with all of Saul's heavy battle gear—and remember,
Saul was a tall man; David was still little more than a boy.

Saul's actions revealed much about the state of his own soul
and his lack of spiritual insight. David knew Goliath could not
be conquered with Saul's armor. David thought quickly and
diplomatically saying he did not have time to test Saul's armor.
Wisely, young David immediately shed Saul's armor. This illustrates a profound truth for all who desire authentic spirituality.

Authentic Spirituality Demands We Shed Saul's Armor

Like David, when we set out on the path of authentic spirituality, we will face opposition. The soul is not a comfortable playground, it is a cosmic battleground. The spiritual war rages on the front line of the human soul. A person can never slay giants—whether they be giants of fear, doubt, temptation, lust, or grief—with "Saul's armor." The prophet Zechariah knew this truth when he declared, "Not by might nor by power, but by My Spirit, says the Lord of Hosts" (Zechariah 4:6).

God never intended for us to fight spiritual battles with Saul's armor. Like David we, too, must shed it. We must let go of an old way of life, for it doesn't fit any more.

A Lesson from Schaeffer

My wife and I are committed to exposing our children to various activities and sports. After pursuing gymnastics for a while, Schaeffer came home and told his mom that he did not want to participate in gymnastics anymore. Liz was a bit surprised by Schaeffer's abrupt decision, so she asked why he felt that way. Schaeffer said, "Mom, it's like an old shoe; it just doesn't fit anymore!"

For the true disciple of Jesus Christ, Saul's armor is like an old shoe—it doesn't fit anymore. As we journey the path to wholeness of soul, layer by layer of Saul's armor must be peeled off and cast aside. Often God gives us the gifts of brokenness and suffering to help us shed Saul's armor. Sometimes He uses other methods. But we can be sure He will use some tool to help us shed the non-spiritual armor we depend upon. We were not meant to wear Saul's armor, but the easy yoke of Christ. Our souls struggle with clinging to Saul's armor.

What Does Saul's Armor Look Like?

King Saul's soul is vividly different than David's. Looking at Saul's tragic life and troubled soul, we can see at least four primary pieces of armor. This is also armor you and I must shed to conquer the giants that keep us from experiencing wholeness of soul in Christ. These pieces of armor are:

> A deceptive self-reliance
> A false sense of security
> A tragic spiritual blindness
> A tormenting soul desperation

A Deceptive Self-Reliance

The first piece of Saul's armor was a deceptive self-reliance. Saul's soul rested on the shifting sands of self. King Saul's strength was in himself and his worldly weapons. Saul's soul was smothered with self-sufficiency and worldly entanglements. What does Saul's armor look like for us? Saul's armor finds strength in human wisdom, prestige, pride, political power, material affluence, financial security, strategic planning, comfort, and success.

Saul's armor looks good on the outside, but it smothers the soul inside. Enamored with the allurements of our culture, many of us have been seduced into wearing Saul's armor. Is it any wonder we are so easily defeated in the battles that rage in our souls? Our seeming ineffectiveness in battling for our culture is directly related to our inability to conquer the battles raging in our own individual souls.

The prophet Jeremiah warned against the dangers of self-reliance. "Let not a wise man boast of his wisdom, and let not the mighty man boast of his might, let not a rich man boast of his riches, but let him who boasts, boast of this, that he understands and knows Me, that I am the Lord who exercises justice and righteousness on the earth for I delight in these things, declares the Lord" (Jeremiah 9:23-24). Self-reliance is a perilous dead end for the soul.

A False Sense of Security

When our children were young, both of them had tenacious attachments to pacifiers. Liz and I felt we might go broke just keeping enough binkies around. Our daughter Sarah was particularly fond of binkies, and if she lost hers in the middle of the night, none of us got any sleep. So we solved the binky crisis by placing several in her crib. We reasoned if she lost the one she was sucking on, she could find another one quickly. Then she wouldn't cry, and we could get our desperately needed sleep.

When we tried to wean Sarah from her binkies, we had little success. I had a nightmare of Sarah going out on her first date with binkies in her hand. Sarah's binky obsession was beginning to loom larger than life.

My brilliant wife solved the problem. She knew Sarah really wanted a doll she had seen at the Disney store. Liz decided to make a deal with Sarah, exchanging her binkies for the doll. Arriving at the store with teary eyes, Sarah clung to her bag of precious binkies. The looming question remained: Would Sarah give up her precious binkies for the doll she so wanted? Bravely, Sarah walked to the checkout counter. Holding the doll in one hand and her bag of binkies in the other hand, she hesitated.

Then mustering up great courage, Sarah handed her mom the bag of binkies she had so cherished.

Thankfully my wife's plan worked. When Sarah found something better, she could say goodbye to her binkies. The nightmare of Sarah taking her binkies on her first date vanished.

Lest we be too hard on Sarah, we must admit that we also have our binkies—things and people that our souls cling to, giving us a false sense of security.

King Saul anchored his soul to the binkies of this world. He clung to his strength, his political position, his charisma, His riches! He was in control. Yet none of these impressive things amounted to much when he faced Goliath. The binkies of this world do not conquer the Goliaths of our soul.

In what do we find our sense of security? The only place of true security is in the everlasting arms of God Himself. Placing our security in anything or anyone else is futile. The prophet Jeremiah uses strong language to remind us, "Cursed is the man who trusts in mankind and makes flesh his strength, and whose heart turns away from the Lord" (Jeremiah 17:5).

A Tragic Spiritual Blindness

The third piece of Saul's armor is a tragic spiritual blindness. The soul smothered in Saul's armor is shrouded from true spiritual vision. Nothing blinds us to the eternal like Saul's armor. King Saul's tragic life is evidence of this. Groping for spiritual insight, crying out for wholeness, grasping for wisdom, King Saul did the unthinkable. He stooped to desperate lows in seeking an occult medium through a pagan spiritist or fortuneteller at Endor.

Saul's desperate soul is a picture of our postmodern age.

Saul's armor can make one religious, but it can never lead the soul to wholeness.

The apostle Paul reminds us to shed Saul's armor and to see reality with true spiritual vision, "While we look not at the things that are seen, but the things that are unseen, for the things that are seen are temporal, but the things that are unseen are eternal" (2 Corinthians 4:18).

When we shed Saul's armor, we begin to see reality as God sees it. We begin to understand the world around us from God's vantage point.

A Soul Full of Despair

The fourth piece of Saul's armor was a tormenting soul of desperation. King Saul's life ended in a downward spiral of despair until he committed suicide by falling on his sword in battle. One of the most insidious aspects of Saul's armor is that we are so used to wearing it, to depending on it, that we are often even unaware that we have it on.

Thoreau captured the peril of a soul smothered in Saul's armor. Most men, Thoreau observed, "live lives of quiet desperation," The tragic end of a soul smothered in Saul's armor is desperation and despair.

How do We know if We Are Wearing Saul's Armor?

If Saul's armor is so deadly, how do we know when we are wearing it? When our hearts are filled with fear and anxiety rather than with faith and hope, we are wearing Saul's armor. When jealousy and selfish ambition fill us instead of humility and love, we are wearing Saul's armor. When we depend more on planning than prayer, we are wearing Saul's armor. When we are enamored with human talent rather than being humbled by God's truth, we are wearing Saul's armor. When religious tradition overshadows biblical truth, we are wearing Saul's armor. When we are hoarding God's resources rather than giving freely, we are wearing Saul's armor. When we embrace our culture's values rather than Scriptural values, we are wearing Saul's armor. When our security is anchored in our financial position rather than our position in Christ, we are wearing Saul's armor. When what we want is more important than what God wants for our lives, we are wearing Saul's armor. One of the great tragedies we see today is the many followers of Jesus Christ whose souls are being smothered in Saul's armor.

Personal Challenge

What giant do you face in the depths of your soul today? Is it a giant of fear? Is it one of doubt? Or perhaps your giant is grief, anger, or bitterness? Is your soul smothered by Saul's armor or surrounded by the armor of God? A soul smothered with Saul's armor can never experience wholeness.

What do we do if we realize our souls are surrounded and smothered by Saul's armor? How do we shed Saul's armor?

Recognize it! Be honest with God and yourself!

Repent and turn from it. Cry to God. Seek his repentance, grace, forgiveness and cleansing.

Begin to peel off Saul's armor by renewing your mind with the truth of God's word. Lay aside every encumbrance!

Lean into the wind of suffering and brokenness. Here God will meet us and we can shed Saul's armor.

Giants Are Not Conquered With Saul's Armor

Few men in history struggled more under the weight of Saul's armor than the great reformer Martin Luther. Luther was familiar with the battle that so often raged in his own soul. Casting aside Saul's armor, Luther penned these timeless words:

> A mighty fortress is our God, A bulwark never failing; Our helper He, amid the flood of mortal ills prevailing. For still our ancient foe doth seek to work us woe; His craft and power are great, and armed with cruel hate, on earth is not his equal. Did we in our own strength confide, our striving would be losing, were not the right Man on our side, the man of God's own choosing: Dost ask who that may be? Christ Jesus, it is He, Lord Saboth His name, from age to age the same, and He must win the battle.

In our journey to wholeness of soul, we will encounter many giants of the soul. Daily we must learn to shed Saul's armor and put on the full armor of God.

> *"Heavenly Father daily remind me of your great faithfulness, mercy and love. Help me to peel off those layers of Saul's armor that encumber and suffocate my soul. Grant me the courage and power to confront the giants that threaten me on the path to wholeness."*

Questions

In this chapter, Tom talks about giants of the soul that torment us. What giants of the soul are you facing?

Fear of failure, personal inadequacy

How does Tom develop his point that the story is primarily

about David's extraordinary insight into spiritual battle and not
merely human courage? Do you find this convincing?

*Using analogy of how David wisely shed
Saul's armor, David refers to "armies of
the living God"*

Who is David referring to when he refers to "the armies of
the living God?" Why is understanding this so important to the
story line?

*The spiritual realm & the armies of Israel
- who serve Almighty God*

Comment on the statement, "Spiritual battles cannot be
won by human weapons."

*They can only be won by
Spiritual weapons*

What other Scriptures support this assertion? (Hint: See
Zechariah 4:6 and Ephesians 6: 10-18)

*Put on the full
armor of God, by God's spirit, by His Word*

The first step in shedding Saul's armor is to identify what it
looks like. What are some of the soul suffocating pieces of
Saul's armor?

*Self reliance, false security,
spiritual blindness
& soul desperation*

Tom tells the story of his daughter Sarah and her attach-
ment to "binkies." What are some "binkies" you are clinging to?
How might the secret of Sarah giving up her "binkies" assist
you in your spiritual journey?

*comfort, control
Jesus's way is always best!*

How do we know if we are wearing Saul's armor?

*When we are caught up in things that
are not of God - fear, anxiety, self
money, the world, our own selfishness*

Using Ephesians 6:10-18, compare and contrast Saul's
armor with the "full armor of God."

*helmet of salvation
Sword of ~~Truth~~ Word of God
Feet fitted w/ readiness that comes from gospel of peace
Belt of Truth   Breastplate of Righteousness
Shield of Faith*

4

Picking Up
The Five Smooth Stones

Train yourself toward godliness [keeping yourself spiritually fit]. For physical training is of some value, but godliness [spiritual training] is useful and of value in everything and in every way, for it holds promise for the present life and also for the life which is to come. 1 Timothy 4:7-8

As we embark on our course of authentic spirituality, we must, as David did, pick up five smooth stones. The five smooth stones are the primary spiritual disciplines that forge vision, power, and wholeness in our souls. Each is an activity within our power that enables us to accomplish what we cannot do by direct effort. These disciplines are critical to being yoked with Jesus—helping us to embrace not only His precepts, but also His practices.

The Foolish Boat Builder

In *The Life God Blesses,* Gordon McDonald relays a parable about a foolish man who built a boat. Now the foolish man wanted his boat to be the best, most beautiful boat that had ever sailed from his boat club. The man worked hard and was a pleasant person, but he had some inner qualities that others in the boat club did not know about.

"As he built, the foolish man outfitted his craft with colorful sails, complex rigging, and comfortable appointments and conveniences in its cabin. The decks were made from beautiful teak-wood; all the fittings were custom-made polished brass. And on the stern, painted in gold letters, readable from a considerable distance was the name of the boat, the *Persona* ....

"Now, and this seems reasonable because no one would ever see the underside of the *Persona*, the man saw little need to be concerned about the boat's keel, or for that matter, anything that had to do with the issue of properly distributed weight or ballast .... everything that would be visible to the people soon began to gleam with excellence. But things that would be invisible when the boat entered the water were generally ignored ....

"When the day came for the boat's maiden voyage, the people of the club joined him at dockside. A bottle of champagne was broken over the bow, and the moment came for the man to set sail. As the breeze filled the sails and pushed the *Persona* from the club's harbor, he stood at the helm and heard what he'd anticipated for years: the cheers and well wishes of envious admirers who said to one another, 'Our club has never seen a grander boat than this. This man will make us the talk of the yachting world' .... But a few miles out to sea a storm arose. Not a hurricane, but not a squall, either. There were sudden wind gusts in excess of forty knots, waves above fifteen feet. The *Persona* began to shudder, and water swept over the sides. Within minutes the *Persona's* colorful sails were in shreds, the splendid mast was splintered in pieces, and the rigging was unceremoniously draped all over the bow. The teakwood decks and the lavishly appointed cabin were awash with water. And then before the foolish man could prepare himself, a wave bigger than anything he'd ever seen hurled down upon the *Persona*, and the boat capsized.

"Now this is important! When most boats would have right-ed themselves after such a battering, the *Persona* did not. Why? Because its builder, this very foolish man, had ignored the importance of what was below the waterline. There was no weight there. The foolish man had concerned himself with the appearance of things and not enough with resilience and stability in the secret, unseen places where storms are withstood.

"The foolish man was never found. Today, when people speak of him—which is rare—they comment not upon the initial success of the man or upon the beauty of his boat but only upon the silliness of putting out on an ocean where storms are sudden and violent. And doing it with a boat that was really never built for anything else but the vanity of the builder and the praise of spectators."[1]

The parable of the foolish man is a sobering reminder to us. We dare not take lightly what lies below the waterline of our lives. That is where a whole and weighty soul is developed, which can withstand perilous storms. Perilous storms threaten to shipwreck our souls on the rocky reefs of agonizing disappointment, severed relationships, financial disaster, gross injustice, heart-wrenching loss, humiliating failure, painful marriages, prolonged singleness, or poor health.

Recently, I received a call from a friend who has suddenly landed in a storm. When I heard his voice, I knew something was very wrong. With a quavering voice he told me he had just found out his wife has a life-threatening illness. As we shared the tears of that moment together, he asked, "Tom, how do those who don't have a strong spiritual anchor make it in life?"

When we face the giants lurking in the shadows of our souls, what is beneath our waterline is revealed. Whether we capsize under the tumult or ride out the storm in triumph depends on the weightiness and wholeness of our souls.

We can clearly see this truth in David's encounter with Goliath, the Philistine giant. In this awe-inspiring story, we find two keys that unlock the door to wholeness of soul.

In the last chapter we discovered the first key found in 1 Samuel 17:39—we must shed Saul's armor. Before going further, I encourage you to read 1 Samuel chapter 17. In this chapter, King Saul insisted that young David wear his armor before tackling the 9'9"giant. "And David girded his sword over his armor and tried to walk, for he had not tested them. So David said to Saul, 'I cannot go with these, for I have not tested them,' and David took them off" (v. 39).

Young David understood what we often miss—giants of the soul are not conquered with worldly weapons. Like David, we must shed Saul's armor. Saul's armor surrounds the soul with a suffocating human pride and a glaring spiritual blindness. Those who truly seek wholeness of soul must shed old ways of life, of thinking, of understanding the world. They must gain new vision and embrace new weapons.

Like David and all those who pursue the path to authentic spirituality, the apostle Paul understood this as well. In his letter to the church at Ephesus, Paul declared, "Finally be strong in the Lord, and in the strength of His might. Put on the full armor of God, that you may be able to stand firm against the schemes of the devil. For our struggle is not against flesh and blood, but against the rulers, against the powers, against the world forces of this darkness, against the spiritual forces of wickedness in the heavenly places. Therefore, take up the full armor of God, that you may be able to resist in the evil day, and having done everything to stand firm, Stand firm … . " (Ephesians 6:10-14).

When David looked at Goliath, he understood the battle was much bigger than a huge, armed-to-the-teeth giant. The battle was clearly cosmic. The fiercest battles ever fought are not on the terra firma of this earth, but on the eternal landscape of the human soul. Battles of bitterness, despair, pride, anger, lust, and temptation require powerful spiritual weapons (2 Cor. 10:3-5).

But David understood that shedding Saul's armor wasn't enough to confront Goliath. David needed the weapons of the wilderness. He needed to pick up the five smooth stones.

We Must Pick Up The Five Smooth Stones

And he took his stick in his hand and chose for himself five smooth stones from the brook, and put them in the shepherd's bag, which he had, even in his pouch, and his sling was in his hand, and he approached the Philistine. Then the Philistine came on and approached David, with the shield-bearer in front of him. When the Philistine looked and saw David, he disdained him, for he was but a youth, and ruddy, with a handsome appearance. And the Philistine said to David, "Am I a dog, that you come to me with sticks?"

And the Philistine cursed David by his gods. The Philistine also said to David, "Come to me, and I will give your flesh to the birds of the sky and the beasts of the field."

Then David said to the Philistine, "You come to me with a sword, a spear, and a javelin, but I come to you in the name of the Lord of hosts, the God of the armies of Israel, whom you have taunted. This day the Lord will deliver you up into my hands, and I will strike you down and remove your head from you. And I will give the dead bodies of the army of the Philistines this day to the birds of the sky and the wild beasts of the earth, that all the earth may know

*that there is a God in Israel. And that all this assembly may
know that the Lord does not deliver by sword or by spear,
for the battle is the Lord's and He will give you into our
hands."*

*Then it happened when the Philistine rose and came
and drew near to meet David, that David ran quickly
toward the battle line to meet the Philistine. And David put
his hand into his bag and took from it a stone and slung it,
and struck the Philistine on his forehead. And the stone sank
into his forehead, so that he fell on his face to the ground.
Thus, David prevailed over the Philistine with a sling and
a stone, and he struck the Philistine and killed him; but
there was no sword in his hand." 1 Samuel 17: 40-50*

David made a very strategic decision. In confronting and
conquering Goliath, he shed the weapons of this world and
picked up the weapons of the wilderness. Man's best military
boot camp didn't prepare David—God's wilderness boot camp
made the difference. David had already embraced some very
special training in the wilderness. God's wilderness training had
built great spiritual vision into David's soul.

The brief dialogue between Goliath and David in verses 41-
47 revealed the soul of both men. David's words captured an
extraordinary vision of the eternal realm and God's angelic
armies. When those around him could only see an imposing
giant, David could only see the awesome power of God and His
angelic armies awaiting the command to invade time and space
and do battle.

A Lesson from Helen Keller

At seven years old, Helen Keller uttered only unintelligible animal sounds. When angry, she would snatch dishes from the table and throw them and herself on the floor. More than one person had told Mrs. Keller that her child was an idiot.

For weeks in the spring of 1887, Annie Sullivan spelled words into Helen's small hand, but could not break through to her consciousness. Then, on April 5, something wonderful happened. Helen Keller described this life-changing moment:

"It happened at the well-house, where I was holding a mug under the spout. Annie pumped water into it, and when the water gushed out into my hand she kept spelling w-a-t-e-r into my other hand with her fingers. Suddenly, I understood. Caught up in the first joy I had known since my illness, I reached out eagerly to Annie's ever-ready hand, begging for new words to identify whatever objects I touched. Spark after spark of meaning flew from hand to hand and miraculously affection was born. From the well-house there walked two enraptured beings calling each other Helen and Teacher."

This watershed event radically changed Helen Keller's life. With this microburst of illuminating insight, she entered an entire new realm of reality. By the time she was 10 years old, Helen Keller had mastered English and French. Then, she quickly mastered five more languages.[ii]

Although history remembers Helen Keller mostly for her heroic achievements, her sense of vision truly stirs the human heart. When asked to comment on the difficulties of being blind, Keller noted that the greatest tragedy in life is not to be blind, but rather to have eyesight and lack vision.

I believe Helen Keller's words are prophetic for our day. One of the greatest tragedies in the church is that while most of us have good temporal eyesight, we lack clear spiritual vision. Immersed in the soul-suffocating morass of materialism, and blinded by the treadmill of busyness, we are often oblivious to the eternal.

"My kingdom is not of this world," Jesus said as He stood before Pilate. Those who would truly follow Jesus must be focused on a kingdom that is not of this world.

A former U.S. Senator commenting on the blindness of our Age said, "If you see in any given situation only what everybody else can see, you can be said to be so much representative of your culture that you are a victim of it."[iii]

Where are the men and women of kingdom vision today— the men and women of God who have the weighty souls needed to conquer giants? Perhaps like David, we must shed Saul's worldly armor and pick up the weapons of the wilderness. It's time we engaged the sling of faith and picked up the five smooth stones.

What are the Five Smooth Stones?

The five smooth stones are the primary spiritual disciplines that forge vision, power, and wholeness in our souls. Being yoked with Jesus Christ in an apprentice relationship means not only that we embrace His teachings, but also that we embrace His practices. Our view of discipleship is often defective because we fail to grasp this point. Discipleship is a distinctive way of life that cultivates our souls. Discipleship is learning to live like Jesus would if He were me. The weapons of the wilderness are central to this distinctive way of life modeled by David and our Lord Jesus.

The five smooth stones build a weighty and whole soul under the waterline of our lives. They are essential for true spiritual transformation. We are often deceived into thinking that spiritual transformation comes as a result of trying harder. The motto of our misunderstanding is like the Avis car rental company motto, "We try harder." But if this is our understanding, we set ourselves up for failure. We must realize the answer is not in trying harder, but in training better!

An Embarrassing Reminder

When a friend and I arrived in Dallas for a conference, we checked into our hotel and had some time to relax before the conference began. We decided to get some badly needed physical exercise in the hotel's weight room. Much of my life I have enjoyed lifting weights and trying to stay in shape, but I must admit that I hadn't been in the weight room very much in quite a while. Most of my upper body exertion had been devoted to pressing keys on my computer keyboard.

Entering the mirrored weight room, I figured I would show my friend I could still pump some serious iron. Stacking a generous portion of weights, I settled on my back ready to begin the bench press. In my macho mind, I figured I would easily press the weights high above my head. Looking in the mirror one last time, I locked my elbows and exhaled. With all of my strength and dreams of yesterday's triumphs, I thrust my arms upward. But there was one problem: Though my mind told my muscles to move the weights, my arms did not move. Neither did the weights. I hadn't even budged the weights on my bench press an inch. Refusing to be conquered, I tried again. No success! To my shock and humiliation I could not even lift the stack on the bench—weights I used to lift with ease.

What happened? My failure was not a result of my desire and effort. No, it was from my lack of disciplined training. My muscles had atrophied, and I had lost a lot of my upper body physical strength. No matter how well intended, no matter how much I tried, I could not lift the weight. My problem became painfully clear. I had lacked the discipline needed for regular training, training that would have allowed me to easily lift this weight.

My appalling experience in the hotel weight room taught me an important spiritual lesson. Like our bodies, our souls need regular exercise. A soul that is not disciplined will atrophy. Spiritual disciplines are exercises for the soul, deepening and strengthening it. These exercises develop a beautiful soul.

Gordon McDonald refers to the spiritual disciplines as the habits of the masters. "I have learned that nothing of value is ever acquired without discipline," McDonald writes. "And so it is with those issues that exist...at soul level. Here it is that one learns to use the words from Thomas a Kempis—to walk inwardly. The spiritual masters have taught us this in every possible way. They have warned us that the one who would get in touch with the soul must do so with diligence and determination. One must overcome feelings, fatigue, distractions, errant appetites, and popular opinion. One must not be afraid of silence, of stillness, or of entering the overpowering presence of divinity with a humble spirit ... . The choice lies in the decision to set aside the necessary time, embrace the habits of the masters, and engage with a waiting God who seeks our communion."[iv]

A Lesson from Tara Lapinski

The best part of the winter Olympic games for our family is

watching the ice skating competition. The grace and skill of these marvelous athletes is breathtaking. As television commentator Vern Lunquist was praising the performance of gold medallist Tara Lapinski, he noted that for many years Tara averaged six hours in training at the rink every day.[v] The key to Tara Lapinski's remarkable triumph was not just trying hard—it was training well!

Why do we understand and applaud the discipline and sacrifice necessary to achieve great athletic prowess, or great artistic mastery, but delude ourselves into thinking that great spiritual mastery and wholeness of soul comes by chance? We seem to think spiritual transformation occurs as a result of some mystic osmosis. Instead, a beautiful soul is a masterpiece built on great concentration and discipline.

The Nelson/Atkins Art Gallery

Liz and I enjoy strolling through museums. One of our favorites is in our hometown, Kansas City. When we wander through the Nelson/Atkins art museum, room after room, we gaze at the magnificent paintings—masterpieces of Monet and Van Gogh and a myriad of other artists.

I must admit that we both lack sophistication in our understanding of art, but this doesn't stop us from standing before these magnificent works of art and admiring their beauty. Oh, the extraordinary talent of the artist's brush! Oh, the delicate nuances of colors and light!

But more than anything else, when I stand before a masterpiece I am absolutely awed by the excruciating work and tenacious discipline that goes into creating any true masterpiece.

When I see a true artistic masterpiece, I remember a

profound spiritual truth. Like a masterpiece of art, a beautiful and whole soul doesn't just happen. A masterpiece of soul, on display for all eternity, is the result of much spiritual discipline.

In our pursuit down the pathway to wholeness of soul, we must not forget the apostle Paul's admonition to his young protégé Timothy!

> *On the other hand, discipline [gymnazio] yourself for the purpose of godliness; for bodily discipline is only of little profit, but godliness is profitable for all things, since it holds promise for the present life and also for the life to come.*

> *1 Timothy 4:7-8*

The word in this verse that is translated "discipline" is the Greek word "gymnazio." We get the English word "gymnasium" from this Greek root. Paul understood the intricate relationship between spiritual exercises and the soul's health and vitality. Why in our culture do we have such a strong emphasis on chiseled bodies, but are content with couch potato souls? Don't soft societies produce soft saints?

"Our attention spans have been conditioned by thirty second commercials," says Eugene Petersen in *A Long Obedience in the Same Direction*. "Our sense of reality has been flattened by thirty-page abridgments ... . In our kind of culture anything, even news about God, can be sold if it is packaged freshly, but when it loses its novelty, it goes on the garbage heap. There is a great market for religious experience in our world; there is little enthusiasm for the patient acquisition of virtue, little inclination to sign up for a long apprenticeship in what earlier generations of Christians called holiness."[vi]

Essential aspects of this apprenticeship, this yoking with Jesus Christ, are the habits of the masters, which are most often referred to as the spiritual disciplines. What is a spiritual discipline? A spiritual discipline is an activity we practice in obedience to Jesus Christ that enables us to accomplish what we cannot do by direct effort.

We must realize we will find no shortcuts to wholeness of soul. We who have embraced Jesus Christ as our Lord and Savior are under grace. We can do nothing to earn our salvation. Salvation is a free gift we must accept by faith in Jesus Christ alone. But we must remember a very important truth. Grace is opposed to merit, not effort. God's grace infuses passion into our effort (Colossians 1:28-29).

Mark McMinn notes, "In the midst of life's hurried and frantic pace, we easily resort to behavioral-management strategies, assuming we can change from the outside in. But in times of quiet, moments of calm, as we set aside life's hurried pace and renew ourselves in God's presence, we recognize that God wants to change us ... . from the inside out. God wants surrender, not sin-management tactics."[vii]

Closing Thoughts

In the 1948 Olympic Games, gifted Czechoslovakian runner, Emil Zatopek won the 10,000-meter race, but lost the 5,000-meter race. He was deeply disappointed and vowed he would win the 5,000-meter race in the 1952 Olympic games.

He trained very hard and realized his goal by winning the 10,000 and 5,000-meter race in the 1952 games. Yet he did not stop there. Even though he had never run a marathon, he entered the marathon at the Olympic games. His strategy was simply to stay with the favored British runner.

Remarkably Zatopek stayed with the British runner until the

18-mile mark, when the British runner tried to psyche out Zatopek by saying, "Is the pace too fast?"

Zatopek responded, "No, the pace is too slow."

Zatopek indeed picked up the pace to leave the favored British runner far behind. As Zatopek entered the Olympic stadium, the massive crowd began to chant, "Zatopek! Zatopek! Zatopek!" Crossing the finish line, Zatopek had not only won the 5,000 and 10,000 meter races, he also won the marathon.

This has never been repeated in Olympic history. Zatopek was asked after the race how he had accomplished such a remarkable achievement. Zatopek answered, "I run and run, until I'm exhausted; then I begin to train."

Wholeness of soul does not come from trying harder, but from training better.

"Now to Him who is able to do exceedingly abundantly beyond all that we ask or think, according to the power that works within us, to Him be the glory in the church and in Christ Jesus to all generations forever and ever. Amen!" (Ephesians 3:20-21)

Questions

What is the compelling life lesson from Gordon Mac-Donald's parable of the foolish boat builder?

Whethe we capsize or ride out the storm depends on the weightiness + wholeness of our soul

What is the importance of God's wilderness training on the path to wholeness of soul?

Because this is where true discipline is forged

What does Tom mean by "the weapons of the wilderness?"

What is a spiritual discipline?

a spiritual discipline is an activity we practice in obedience to Jesus Christ that enables us to accomplish what we cannot do by our own direct effort

What do spiritual disciplines accomplish?

Helps us train better

What are the five smooth stones, and how do they synergistically work together? *The primary spiritual disciplines*

Prayer, Bible study

Why is the Avis car rental motto, "We just try harder" such a deadly deception in the spiritual arena?

Because grace is opposed to merit not effort Trying harder doesn't get results - training better does

How would my daily life be different if I truly embraced "training better with the Master and not merely trying harder?" *see successes build confidence in God + what He is doing in you + through you.*

How do the necessities for a physically fit body relate to the realities needed for a spiritually fit soul?

It is all about the training regimen.

What is the significance of the Apostle Paul's use of the Greek word "gymnazio" in 1 Timothy 4:7?

Comment on Mark McMinn's pithy statement, "God wants surrender, not sin management tactics." How have you substituted sin management tactics for surrender?

5

The Smooth Stone of Solitude

And after He had dismissed the multitudes, He went up into the hills by Himself to pray. When it was evening, He was still there alone. Matthew 14:23

Once a pastor's integrity was tested greatly regarding two very wealthy brothers who lived in his community. Both brothers were self-absorbed scoundrels who seldom darkened a church door. Then one day, one of the wealthy brothers died.

Much to the pastor's surprise the surviving brother showed up at his door. The brother got right to the point. "Pastor, I know you need a lot of money for the new church building," he said. "In this envelope is a check for a million dollars I will give to you if you will hold my brother's funeral. But I have one stipulation. When you do the funeral, I want you to tell everybody he was a saint."

The pastor agreed and deposited the check in the church account. The church was overflowing with people attending the wealthy brother's funeral. Then the time came for the pastor to speak.

Much to everyone's shock, the pastor announced, "I want you know that our dear departed brother was one of the most

selfish, rude, greedy, lying, cheating people in this community …
but compared to his brother, he was a real saint!"

We chuckle at this pastor's cleverness, but at this stage in our
journey, each of us needs to realize that an integral life is not a
perfect life. Wholeness of soul is not perfectionism. It is not a
human-centered sainthood. Rather, it is an authentic life in Jesus
Christ—one that is modeled after Christ and filled with spiritual discipline, including the discipline of solitude.

What Is the Discipline of Solitude?

Dallas Willard defines the discipline of solitude as "electing
to step free from human relationships for a lengthy period of
time, in isolation or anonymity, to make room for occupation of
our lives by God."[i]

Jeanne Guyon in her seventeenth century classic, *Experiencing The Depths Of Jesus Christ,* captures the essence of solitude
when she comments, "What does it mean to give your whole
heart to God? To give your whole heart to God is to have all the
energy of your soul always centered on Him."[ii]

In other words, the discipline of solitude focuses the energy
of one's soul on Jesus alone. When we talk about solitude, we are
not talking about loneliness. Often the fear of being alone petri-
fies people. Why? Because loneliness is an inner emptiness;
whereas, solitude is inner fulfillment.

Henry David Thoreau, who was not sympathetic to Christianity, stumbled onto the very real substance of solitude. During two years of solitude at Walden Pond, Thoreau wrote, "I
have never found the companion that was so companionable as
solitude."[iii]

Solitude for the Christian is not primarily about getting away from people, but about hearing God better. It is not about personality extroversion or introversion, but about spiritual transformation.

On a Personal Note

One highlight of our parental odyssey is to tuck our children in bed at night. While some nights include a struggle of wills, I will always treasure other special moments. One of those moments was when Schaeffer, who was then seven years old, finished his bedtime prayers.

Listening to Schaeffer pray, I was deeply moved by his authenticity and insight. Giving him a big smile, I looked into his eyes and said, "Schaeffer, you not only have a great mind, you also have a very beautiful soul." A bit embarrassed at my comment, he looked at me and said, "You're such a corny old guy, Dad!"

Perhaps all this talk about wholeness of soul and the spiritual disciplines makes you feel a bit like my son Schaeffer and you're thinking, "You're such a corny old guy! Are you kind of going off the deep end here? Is this stuff really on target?"

How Did Jesus Embrace the Discipline of Solitude?

As we mentioned before, our view of discipleship is often defective. We think if we can just try harder, we can do better and please God more. But our need is not to try harder, but to train better. We must learn to live like Jesus would if He were us.

Did Jesus practice the discipline of solitude? Was this an important aspect of His life and ministry?

Let's scan the timeless terrain of the Gospels. In Matthew, we see Jesus practicing the discipline of solitude. In chapter four, before the beginning of His ministry, we read, "Then Jesus was led up by the Spirit into the wilderness to be tempted by the devil. And after forty days and forty nights, He became hungry. And the tempter came and said to Him, 'If You are the Son of God, command that these stones become bread'" (Matthew 4:1-3).

Often we think of the wilderness as a place of deprivation or temptation. We have the idea that Satan wanted to isolate Jesus and neutralize Him before He launched His ministry. But Matthew clearly reveals that after forty days of fasting, the evil one came to Jesus. What, then, is the point of this text?

The Spirit led Jesus into the wilderness to prepare Him for the temptation He would later encounter. The wilderness was not primarily a place of temptation, but of solitude. In this place, Jesus could exercise and strengthen the soul.

The Holy Spirit, much like the manager of a prizefighter, isolates the prizefighter from the distractions of the world and puts the fighter through an intense training regimen to prepare him for the big fight. In this scripture, the Holy Spirit put Jesus, the God-man, through spiritual conditioning. The discipline of solitude was an essential aspect of Jesus' preparation.

Matthew also records that in the middle of Jesus' ministry, with all of its demands, He practiced the discipline of solitude. Matt. 14:23 tells us, "And after He had sent the multitudes away, He went up to the mountain by Himself to pray, and when it was evening, He was there alone." Jesus disciplined Himself to practice the discipline of solitude in the midst of a hectic schedule.

At the end of His earthly ministry, Jesus, preparing for the cross, entered the discipline of solitude and prayer in the Garden of Gethsemane. The discipline of solitude was an integral part of Jesus' earthly life.

The Gospel of Mark also records Jesus regularly practicing the discipline of solitude. Mark 1:35 tells us, "And in the early morning, while it was still dark, He arose and went out and departed to a lonely place and was praying there." Since the sun rises over Jordan's foothills very early, Jesus was probably up at 4 or 5 a.m.

One of my fondest memories is the summer my wife and I spent on a graduate study program in Israel. As a part of this study program, we lived in the Old City of Jerusalem. One routine I quickly embraced was rising early and jogging around the Old City. I immediately noticed how light it was for so early in the morning. To climb to the top of Mount Scopus, on the Eastern side of Jerusalem, and catch the sun rising over the Jordanian Hills, I had to get out of bed very early. As I enjoyed delightful solitude on Mount Scopus waiting for the sunrise, I often wondered what it must have been like for Jesus to get up so early to enjoy invigorating times of solitude with the Heavenly Father. Yet this invigorating time demanded great personal discipline from the Son of God. Solitude may not demand our getting out of bed at 4 a.m., but it does require great discipline and intentional planning.

Jesus not only modeled the discipline of solitude, He encouraged His disciples to seek solitude. In Mark 6:31, Jesus told His disciples, "Come away by yourselves to a lonely place and rest a while. For there were many people coming and going, and they did not even have time to eat."

In the Gospel of Luke we also see the practice of solitude. Luke 4:42 reveals, "And when day came, He departed and went to a lonely place ... ." Luke 5:16 notes, "But He Himself would often slip away to the wilderness and pray."

For Jesus and all of us who want to follow him, the discipline of solitude is essential for wholeness of soul. We must understand that grace is opposed to earning, not effort. We cannot merit any favor from God by *doing*, but we are to follow Jesus with all of our *being*.

The scriptures also show us the discipline of solitude practiced in the lives of Moses, David, Joseph, and Paul. In 2000 years of history, the church of Jesus Christ follows a long line of God's people who filled their lives with spiritual disciplines. Throughout the history of the church, the spiritual disciplines have been considered an indispensable facet of the normal Christian life.

Only in recent times have the disciplines been dismissed as extreme, or cast aside as superfluous. This has hurt both the individual souls and the church of Jesus Christ. Truly this is a perilous blind spot of the modern church. The spiritual disciplines are not reserved for some ascetic monk sitting on a pole in the wilderness for 30 years, or only for those with seminary degrees. Rather, the spiritual disciplines are to mark every follower of Jesus Christ. They are an indispensable part of being yoked with Jesus Christ.

An Example in Dawson Trotman

Few people have influenced me more than Dawson Trotman, the founder of the Navigators. As a teenager I read his biography, and although I never met him, his love for God and his commitment to discipleship deeply affected my soul. A couple of years ago our family spent two days at Glen Erie, the beautiful Colorado headquarters of the Navigator ministry.

Soon after we arrived, I found the trail that led to Trotman's grave. The trail takes you in the foothills overlooking the breathtaking canyon in which Glen Erie sits. Dawson had often gone to this place alone to pray. As I sat near his grave, I realized this was surely one of the keys to Dawson Trotman's extraordinary life—he had a place where his thirsty soul was satisfied, where his soul was strengthened, where he picked up the smooth stone of solitude.

My Personal Journey

Although I grew up in a Christian family, attended a Bible-believing church, was a Christian for 30 years, and had pastored for several years, I never understood or embraced the discipline of regular solitude until a few years ago. Somehow I was under the deceptive impression that solitude was reserved for a monastic life. I had good intentions, but a defective understanding of what it meant to be a disciple of Jesus Christ. Once I understood solitude, this discipline entirely changed my life and my walk with Christ. Why is solitude so important? What are its benefits?

What Are the Benefits of Solitude?

Solitude Frees Our Soul From Hurtful Entanglements

Hebrews 12:1-2 encourages, "Therefore since we have so great a cloud of witnesses surrounding us, let us also lay aside every encumbrance, and the sin which so easily entangles us, and let us run with endurance the race that is set before us, fixing our eyes on Jesus, the author and perfecter of our faith...."

Through the discipline of solitude we free ourselves from the burdens and entanglements of the world. We find we can live without others and they without us. The world does not rest on our shoulders. Dallas Willard emphasized, "In solitude we find the psychic distance, the perspective from which we can see, in the light of eternity, the created things that trap, worry, and oppress us."[iv]

Andrew Murray wrote, "The desert initiates us into the life of the spirit by helping us discover who we most deeply are. To follow Christ means that we must let go of excessive attachments to passing pleasures and possessions, to ploys of autonomous power, to tangible goods as if they were ultimate. Christ asks us to abandon our idols, whatever they may be, and to love Him with our entire being."[v]

King David captured this truth in Psalm 23 as he wrote, "The Lord is my Shepherd, I shall not want He makes me lie down in green pastures He leads me beside quiet waters. He restores my soul."

What entangles your soul? Is it a person? Is it some thing?

In solitude our soul is restored. Solitude caresses our souls with the fresh breezes of eternity.

Solitude Also Breaks the Merciless Tyranny of Time

It is time we get off the treadmill of the hectic pace of our lives. The discipline of solitude helps us do this. In solitude, we discover the barrenness of busyness. I've heard that humans are the only creatures on this planet that when lost go faster. Solitude is like a compass; it reorients our souls and sets us in the right direction. Solitude enables clarity and resolution of purpose and strength to avoid distraction in our lives.

The Discipline of Solitude Allows Us to Cultivate a deep Intimacy with Jesus Christ

King David used the metaphor of a weaned child with his or

her mother to describe the delightful intimacy he shared with God in times of solitude. In Psalm 131, we read, "O Lord, my heart is not proud, nor my eyes haughty; nor do I involve myself in great matters, or in things too difficult for me. Surely I have stilled and quieted my soul like a weaned child rests against his mother, like a weaned child is my soul within me."

What a remarkable picture of intimacy and contentment David expressed. David also expressed his soul in solitude in Psalm 46:10, "Be still [cease striving, NASB] and know that I am God ... ."

When we pick up the smooth stone of solitude, we choose to be with God in a way that is different from when we focus on human relationships or temporal tasks. In solitude, we hear God's gentle whisper.

Fenelon, a beautiful soul in church history, wrote, "How rare it is to find a soul quiet enough to hear God speak."[vi] In the invigorating silence of solitude, the echoes of kingdom reality shout in our soul.

In his book *The Coming World Revival*, Robert Coleman writes, "God's people everywhere increasingly yearn for something more in the life of the church. We go through the motions of religion, but there is no power. For many the thrill of personal devotion is gone. The joy of the Lord has leaked out; there is no spring in our step, no shout in our soul."[vii]

I suggest the reason our souls express so little shout is that we have not picked up the five smooth stones of spiritual discipline.

The Discipline of Solitude Enhances the Other Spiritual Disciplines

Solitude is the soul's backdrop where the other disciplines

come into full focus. Bible study, prayer and fasting nurture the mind and soul best in the soil of solitude. Solitude is the soil in which the eternal truths of Scripture flourish. In the rich soil of solitude, we find a whole new depth and dimension of prayer. Solitude is the garden of the soul.

Solitude is the womb where spiritual insight is conceived where God's word has time to germinate and flourish. This is why solitude is such a foundational spiritual discipline. The discipline of solitude is essential for wholeness of soul and spiritual transformation. Is solitude beneficial to the soul? Yes. Even under very difficult circumstances.

A Lesson in Alexander Solzhenitsyn

Alexander Solzhenitsyn, a Russian dissident who spent many years in a Soviet Gulag, writes about the forced solitude of his prison life, "It was only when I lay there on rotting prison straw that I sensed within myself the first stirrings of good. Gradually, it was disclosed to me that the line separating good and evil passes, not through states, nor between classes, nor between political parties either, but right through every human heart, and through all human hearts. So bless you, prison, for having been in my life."[viii]

The discipline of solitude is not only beneficial, it is essential for spiritual transformation.

How Do We Begin To Practice Solitude?

Evaluate and Adjust Your Priorities

We all have enough time for what is truly important to us. The discipline of solitude will squeeze out other good activities in your life. Something else will have to go, but it will be worth it!

"Tom, you must concentrate and eliminate!" are my wife's favorite words when I find my schedule getting too packed. Her wisdom is right on track. To build the discipline of solitude, you will have to eliminate some good things in your life.

Create Margin In Your Lifestyle

Margin is simply what you have left over after all your commitments. Marginless living fills our culture. To regain a margin of time and financial resources we must be courageous enough to swim upstream against the cultural current. We must make lifestyle changes that allow time for solitude.

Marginless living erodes our joy, hinders our relationships, and squeezes the very life from our souls. It is a silent and insidious killer. We must concentrate on the truly important and eliminate the rest to create spare time.

Schedule Time for Solitude

In our busy, scheduled lives, we must plan ahead for solitude and then guard that time. In your home begin to model the discipline of solitude for your children. We do this with Schaeffer and Sarah by giving them a regular time to play or read alone in their rooms without interaction with others.

Think about the importance of the Sabbath in your home. Discern the difference between leisure and rest from a soul perspective. Leisure is designed to renew the body. Biblical rest is designed to renew the soul as well. Find a time and place for regular solitude. Learn to walk to the Master's cadence, embracing a lifestyle rhythm of engagement and withdrawal.

Start Small and Work Your Way Up

I love the title of a recently released book by Cathy Lechner, *I'm Trying To Sit At His Feet, But Who's Going To Cook Dinner?*

Understand the unique limitations and opportunities of your particular life cycle. Discover if solitude works best for you in the middle of the night, early morning, or during travel times.

Seize small moments. Begin with an hour over lunch at a park; then try an afternoon, a day, a weekend of solitude! I encourage you to look over your schedule for this week right now and block in some time for solitude. Even in the most difficult circumstances, we can embrace the discipline of solitude.

Closing Thoughts

Not long ago, a conference of Christ-followers was held in England. At one meeting a Chinese pastor who had spent eighteen years in prison for his faith gave his testimony to the assembled people. He recalled his prison experience with these words:

"My friends wonder what kind of work I did in the labor camp to keep me physically healthy. I answered them that life in the labor camp was very, very hard. The authorities in the camp put me to emptying the human waste cesspool.

"Most prisoners were afraid to approach the cesspool, but the authorities were aware of my background—I was well educated, from a well-to-do family. But because they were atheists, they were even more interested in the fact that I was a Christian leader. So they enjoyed putting me to work in the human waste cesspool. What they did not know in those years, however, was how I enjoyed working there.

"It was more than two meters in breadth and two meters in length, filled with human waste collected from the entire camp. Once it was full, the human waste was kept until it was ripe and then dug out and sent to the field as fertilizer. Because the pit was so deep, I could not reach the bottom to empty it, so I had to walk into the disease-ridden mass and scoop out the successive layers of human waste, all the time breathing the strong stench.

"The guards and all the prisoners kept a long way off because of the stench. So why did I enjoy working in the cesspool? I enjoyed the solitude. In the labor camp all the prisoners normally were under strict surveillance and no one could be alone. But when I worked in the cesspool, I could be alone and could pray to our Lord as loudly as I needed. I could recite the Scriptures, including all the Psalms I still remembered, and no one was close enough to protest. That's the reason I enjoyed working in the cesspool. Also, I could sing loudly the hymns I still remembered.

"In those days one of my favorite hymns was 'In the Garden.' Before I was arrested, this was my favorite hymn, but at that time I did not realize the real meaning of this hymn. When I worked in the cesspool, I knew and discovered a wonderful fellowship with our Lord. Again and again I sang this hymn and felt our Lord's presence with me.

I come to the garden alone, while the dew is still on the roses;
And the voice I hear falling on my ear, the Son of God discloses.
And He walks with me and he talks with Me, and he tells me I am His own,
And the joy we share as we tarry there, none other has ever known.

"Again and again as I sang this hymn in the cesspool, I experienced the Lord's presence. He never left me or forsook me. And so I survived, and the cesspool became my private garden."[ix]

Picking Up The Smooth Stone of Solitude

Remember solitude is not about doing, but about being. The goal is not to "wisely use your time." We are not seeking productivity, but intimacy with Jesus Christ. Solitude is an intentional decision to get off the treadmill of a busy life and make room for God in our lives. As the Psalmist reminds us, our goal is to "Cease striving and know that He is God (Psalm 46:10). When we enter solitude, our focus is to give our whole heart to God and to fix the energy of our soul on Christ. In the garden of solitude we seek a deeper communion with our Lord Jesus Christ.

For many of us, the spiritual discipline of solitude is a new concept. The question that comes to our minds is, "Where do I begin?" Here is a summary of ideas to help you overcome your initial inertia.

Some Helpful Tips

Start small and work your way up. Begin by carving out an hour or two to engage your soul in the discipline of solitude.

Find an appropriate place for solitude. Solitude demands that we extricate ourselves from other human relationships and worldly distractions. This means we seek a place where we will not be interrupted and where we will be as free as possible from noise. I have found that to get as close to nature as possible is the best backdrop for solitude.

Psalm 19 reminds us the "heavens declare the glory of God."

Take some time initially to let your mind wind down. I do not mean you should empty your mind, for that is a pagan and dangerous form of meditation. But give yourself time for your heart and mind to quiet down.

Engage in a time of worship. I suggest that you bring a Bible with you and a hymnal or songbook. Praise God for all that you see around you. Praise God for the truths of Holy Scripture and the great plan of salvation. Review some memory verses.

Embrace an extended time of stillness. Here you allow God to commune with your soul. I have found that God often brings to mind a passage of scripture or a truth from general revelation to impress me on a deeper level than I have known before. God does not audibly speak to me. But His communion is very real and clear.

End your time of solitude with journaling. I have found it meaningful at times to write what I have discovered in my time of solitude.

Add other disciplines to solitude. Solitude is such a foundational spiritual discipline because it is the soil from which other disciplines grow. As you grow in your solitude, you will want to integrate other disciplines like prayer, fasting and study.

In the "garden of solitude" our precious Lord Jesus awaits our fellowship!

"In the invigorating garden of solitude, Jesus awaits your fellowship. The greatest lover of your soul longs for intimacy with you! He who believes in Me, from his inner-most being shall flow rivers of living water." John 7:38

Questions

What is the spiritual discipline of solitude?

Choosing to be free of human relationships for a lengthy period of time in isolation or anonymity to make room for the occupation of Jesus by God

What role did the discipline of solitude play in Jesus' earthly life and ministry? (Give biblical references.)

Matt 4:13 spent 40 days in wilderness preparing for ministry, Matt 14:23 prayed in mountains, mark 1:35 Got up early to pray alone

How does Psalms 131 capture the essence of the discipline of solitude? What truths can you glean from the metaphor of a weaned child with its mother?

stilled + quieted my soul
picture of contented child resting in it's mother's lap

Tom asserts, "Solitude is the womb where spiritual insight is conceived." How have you seen this reality woven into the tapestry of your spiritual life?

you can hear God better

What are some obstacles to practicing the discipline of solitude?

Busyness
Too many good things

What are some practical ways to begin practicing the discipline of solitude?

start small then expand + build

What does Tom suggest when he says that as Jesus' apprentices, we must begin to walk to the cadence of the Master, embracing a lifestyle of engagement and withdrawal?

How does the discipline of solitude relate to enhancing other spiritual disciplines? *When you cultivate solitude you are laying the groundwork for other discipling*

Briefly share the joys and challenges of a time when you entered the discipline of solitude.

6

The Smooth Stone of Prayer

*And in the morning, long before daylight, He got up
and went out to a deserted place, and there He prayed.*
Mark 1:35

One of my greatest handicaps in life is working with my
hands. As a husband and a father I am aware that building and
fixing things comes with the turf. And I do try to overcome
being manually challenged, but I am haunted by many painful,
embarrassing memories.

I knew I was in trouble when a neighbor in our cul-de-sac
began to build an elaborate wood playhouse and swing set for
his children. After playing for only an afternoon in this wonder
built of wood, my children bounded in the door bursting with
the passionate enthusiasm reserved for discovering "Disney
World®" next door.

"Dad, will you build us a fort like that in our backyard,
please, please Dad?" they begged. And when I could not hide the
shock and terror from my face any longer, rather than backing
off, they continued to press the issue further. With Liz watching
and the flashing of "Bad Dad" highlighted behind my eyeballs, I
was clearly cornered—trapped between the rock of fear and the

hard place of guilt. My children had clearly pinned me to the mat!

Reluctantly, I went to the local building supply store. When I admitted that I was manually challenged and lacked experience for such a gargantuan task, the salesman assured me he had just what I needed—it was a building kit for dads just like me with all the lumber precut and the hardware included, along with several pages of "easy do-it-yourself" instructions. Taking my credit card and giving me a pat on the back, the smiling salesman sent me out of the store the proud owner and future builder of the "Eagle's Nest." With a name like "Eagle's Nest" I should have known some very large challenges loomed ahead. Intuitively, I knew "turkeys" don't build "eagle's nests."

When I told a friend my anxiety about building the Eagle's Nest, he sensed my desperation and volunteered to help me put this together. Saturday morning arrived, and we met in my backyard, pieces of wood scattered all over the lawn and pages of directions flapping in the breeze. Our task was to build the swing set, which seemed to be less complicated than the playhouse. The directions assured that we only needed a few socket wrenches to tighten the bolts, and an electric drill to make holes through the large wood supports and crossbar.

I began to panic when I realized I didn't own an electric drill, but then my friend said, "Tom, I just got a new electric drill that I have not even used yet." Quickly, he disappeared. Then he came back with a beaming smile, tightly gripping a shiny, new electric drill. With confidence and enthusiasm exuding from his every pore, my friend blurted out, "Here, let's give this baby a try!"

After placing a special wood-boring bit into the drill, we measured the large crossbeam from which the swings would be suspended. Next, it was time to let this baby rip! I grabbed the drill, placed the bit dead center on the marking and pulled the trigger. The bit turned and I pressed down on the drill. Slowly, the bit penetrated the six-inch-wood beam. Beads of sweat poured down my face as I continued to exert pressure on the drill. It seemed as if the bit would never get through the wood.

I had only made a little progress when I had to take a break! My friend grabbed the drill and continued what I had begun. Soon, we both felt frustrated and exhausted! Finally, the drill bit penetrated the six-inch beam. As if we were two football players who had just scored a touchdown, we stopped to celebrate, giving each other high fives for such a stunning accomplishment.

However, our celebration was short-lived when we realized seven other holes still needed to be completed. At that moment, we both knew it would be a long morning.

I don't know what made me look closer at the drill, but suddenly I noticed a little red button near the drill's trigger! I thought, "I wonder what this is for?"

I asked my friend if he knew what the little red button did. He shrugged his shoulders. Like me, he was clueless! So I did what every clueless person does—I pushed the little red button and then pulled the trigger. Instantly, I felt a surge of amazing power. I felt like I had a jackhammer in my hand. The electric drill was suddenly turbo-charged. This was the kind of power I had been looking for!

With renewed confidence, I placed the drill bit on the next marking and pulled the trigger. The drill cut through the wood as if I was drilling through soft butter! In a few seconds, the drill bit had effortlessly left a perfect hole in the six-inch beam. What had been a pain in the neck now became a piece of cake. I had discovered the little red button—the button that gave the drill the power needed to accomplish its purpose.

My experience with the electric drill parallels my spiritual journey. For so long I pursued the path to authentic spirituality, but had not discovered the little red button of prayer. One of the greatest challenges to wholeness of soul is the ever-increasing need to grow deeper in our conversation with God.

Most of us find prayer is a challenge. No matter where we are in our spiritual journey, we feel inadequate in understanding and embracing the mystery of prayer. Prayer is often a deep, soul-level struggle.

If I asked you how many minutes a day you think a pastor spends in prayer, what would you answer? Dr. Peter Wagner conducted a survey of 572 American pastors to find out just how much time they spend in prayer. Dr. Wagner concluded:[i]

> 57% of pastors pray less than 20 minutes a day
> 34% pray between 20 minutes and 1 hour a day
> 9 % pray 1 hour or more a day
> The average prayer time was 22 minutes daily
> 1 out of 4 prayed less than 10 minutes a day

Prayer is an ongoing struggle even for those who are "paid to be good." Few things have been a greater struggle in my life than the consistent discipline of prayer. My struggle is not due to a lack of information—I have more books on prayer in my library than on almost any other topic. Too often, I rationalize superficial "touch and go landings" with God on the basis of my "busy schedule." Oh, the barrenness of busyness!

Bedtime Prayers

When my children were young, Liz and I would always tuck

them in at bedtime. Usually, we would have some pillow talk about the day. Then, part of this bedtime ritual was praying with our children and listening to them say their prayers. How I cherish memories of our children's bedtime prayers! What a joy to peer into the windows of their young souls. Sometimes their prayers brought us to quiet tears, and at other times they gave us roaring laughter. But at times, because of fatigue, Schaeffer and Sarah would put their prayers in high speed. Simply going through the motions, their weary bodies and busy minds totally disengaged from meaningful conversation with God.

Yet rather than looking at their high-speed prayers judgmentally, I found in them a sobering reflection of my own prayer life.

So often I catch myself just going through the motions with high-speed prayers, stopping only long enough to alleviate my guilt of prayerlessness; simply trying to quickly touch bases with God while my mind is bombarded with distractions and mental "to do" lists. At times when I'm on my knees praying, I cannot seem to concentrate, either because I am so tired or because my mind will not stop racing long enough for me to enter intimate moments with the Greatest Lover of my soul.

At other times, I grow weary and fainthearted, when I've prayed for something for a long time and God doesn't seem to be hearing me. My prayers feel like they are bouncing off the ceiling.

In talking with many others, I have discovered that the discipline of prayer is also a great struggle of their souls. Dallas Willard writes, "The open secret of many Bible believing churches is that a vanishingly small percentage of those talking about prayer...are actually doing what they are talking about." [ii]

No matter where we are in our spiritual pilgrimage, we must

very good

grow in our understanding and practice of prayer. Prayer is to the soul what oxygen is to the body; without it, true spirituality cannot be sustained. The great pioneer missionary William Carey once said, "Prayer, secret, fervent, believing prayer lies at the root of all personal godliness."[iii]

Prayer, like light, is an undeniable reality of the universe, yet one of reality's greatest mysteries. Few have even begun to plumb its divine depths.

Why Is Prayer So Often a Struggle?

If God wants us to have an intimate relationship with Him through prayer, why is praying so often a battle in our lives? Let me suggest three primary reasons why we struggle:

Prideful self-reliance

Crippling caricatures

Spiritual warfare

Prideful Self-reliance

In *Too Busy Not To Pray,* Pastor Bill Hybels addresses the core issue of our prayerlessness. He writes, "From birth we have been learning the rules of self-reliance as we strain and struggle to achieve self-sufficiency. Prayer flies in the face of those deep-seated values. It is an assault on human autonomy, an indictment of independent living. To people in the fast lane, determined to make it on their own, prayer is an embarrassing interruption."[iv]

Why is prayer often a struggle? Because it is alien to our proud human nature! Those who pray the least, rely on themselves the most.

Crippling Caricatures

Because of biblical ignorance, our religious traditions, or our past spiritual experiences, we can easily develop a distorted picture of prayer. Sometimes we think of God as a cosmic butler, a sort of "gimme, gimme" God who is waiting to fulfill our latest whim or desire. We approach God like a vending machine—just put in the coins and out come the goodies. We think if we say just the right prayer, mustering up enough faith and sincerity, we will receive just what we want. And when we don't receive exactly what we want when we want it, we pout or conclude, "Well, I guess this God and prayer thing does not work."

Because God is a good and loving God, He often grants us what our hearts desire, but He is not a cosmic butler. His ways and purposes are much beyond this!

Sometimes we think of God as a cosmic therapist. Our prayers are mostly "owee" prayers! When we approach God, it's with a physical or emotional pain we ask Him to take away. And if He doesn't take all the pain away, we conclude that God must not hear us or doesn't really care about our hurts.

Because God is a good and loving God, He often heals our pains. But He is not a cosmic therapist—His purposes go far beyond this. In fact, He often, instead of healing our pains, uses them for greater growth in our lives. C.S. Lewis said, "Pain is often God's megaphone to arouse a lost and dying world."

Sure, at times God intervenes in our lives by healing our pain or granting our desires, but prayer is more than a hotline to heaven. Prayer involves asking, but it is so much more than a pragmatic means to get what we want. We must cast aside these devastating caricatures of prayer. Prayer is a transforming friendship. It is an ongoing intimate conversation with God about what we are doing together with Him.

Spiritual Warfare

When the United States and the United Nations Coalition drove Saddam Hussein out of Kuwait in the Desert Storm War, I was interested to find that their top priority was to destroy Iraq's command and control system. Using the most sophisticated technology, the allied forces attacked Iraq's communication system. Once this was eliminated, the allies mopped up the Iraqi army in only a matter of time. This illustrates a powerful principle of warfare: If you destroy your enemy's communication system, you cripple their military machine.

The Bible reveals that a much greater war is being waged—an invisible war of cosmic proportions! In describing this spiritual warfare in Ephesians 6, Paul tells us to put on the whole armor of God. After listing the various pieces of armor, it is not by accident or coincidence that he concludes with a strong exhortation to prayer.

Satan's top priority is to keep us from communicating with God and to keep us from developing intimacy with God. Is it any wonder then that in the discipline of prayer, the spiritual battle for our soul rages with hell's greatest fury? We must remember that Satan laughs at our well-designed strategies, but he trembles when he sees the weakest disciple of Jesus on his knees.

Although a growing and vibrant prayer life will always be a struggle, each of us can and must make progress in prayer. Jesus modeled an authentic and vibrant prayer life for us.

Some Important Observations

Jesus' Prayer Life was a Discipline

The Gospel writers give special attention to Jesus' prayer life. For example, at the beginning of Jesus' ministry, Mark notes that despite many demands, Jesus kept his discipline of prayer as a top priority. Mark 1:35 illustrates, "And in the early morning, while it was still dark, He arose and went out and departed to a lonely place, and was praying there."

Let's look at the context preceding this verse. Jesus had been up very late the night before ministering to people. I am sure he was physically and emotionally exhausted by the time he got to sleep. Yet he arose very early—even while it was still dark. He was up before anybody else was up. And the fact that his disciples found Him suggests that they knew His pattern of life.

This wasn't an isolated incident. Luke reminds us of this in Luke 5:16, "But He [Jesus] Himself would often slip away to the wilderness to pray."

I am sure it wasn't easy for Jesus to get up for prayer, but this time was so important that nothing could get in its way, not even sleep. We all have enough time to do what is most important to us. The discipline of prayer was a top priority for Jesus and must be a top priority for us. Jesus' discipline of prayer was combined with other spiritual disciplines such as solitude, silence and fasting.

Woody Allen said that 90 percent of life is just showing up. Well, in many ways, 90 percent of prayer is the consistent discipline to simply show up. We show up to meet with God not just when we are in crisis or when we feel like it.

Ben Patterson gets to the heart of prayer when he writes,

"Prayer is a discipline before it is a joy, and remains a discipline even after it becomes a joy."[V]

Getting on the Path to Getting in Shape

As a kid, I loved sports of all kinds. Wrestling was my favorite sport and became a constant pastime for me. I loved the intensity of the mat, the one-on-one, head-to-head competition. And though it demanded a lot of physical training, I really didn't mind the long practices in a hot, sweaty wrestling room. My intensity to win even led me to do what I had previously concluded was the unthinkable—going out for the cross-country team.

Running on the cross-country team in high school made me conclude two important things. First, I realized I was not a runner. As a wrestler, I looked much more like an army tank lumbering down the road than a graceful runner striding toward the finish line. Second, I realized just how much I detested running—that is until I went to college.

During my first year in college, a friend who loved to run and ran what I considered an unbelievable amount of miles, kept bugging me about running. I kept putting him off with excuses. Finally, my friend convinced me to give running another try. And sure enough, after class he showed up at my dorm room all pumped up about getting me to pound the pavement.

I will never forget how helplessly out of shape I felt trying to keep up with this guy. Completely out of breath, with my sides aching, I finally stopped after running just a mile. I was convinced my running experiment was history. My friend, however, had other ideas. A sanguine encourager, he slapped me on the back and enthusiastically said, "Great job for the first day! I'll stop by your dorm room tomorrow and we'll have at it again."

I had no doubt in my mind that he would show up at my dorm room the next day. And he did! But something happened in the following days. Running began to hurt less and I was able to go farther distances. As my cardiovascular efficiency improved, I surprisingly began to look forward to my daily run. Rather than drudgery, running became a delight. Over the years, jogging has become a vital part of my lifestyle. The seeds of discipline have produced the delicious fruits of joy in my life.

My experience with the spiritual discipline of prayer has been a lot like my experience with running. On some days, the last thing I want to do is go out and pound the pavement—yet once I embrace the discipline and take the first few steps, it becomes an exhilarating delight. The joy I experience in prayer flows from a regular commitment to make the time and get on my knees and "just do it!"

Jesus' Prayer Life Was Compelling

In Luke 11:1 we read, "And it came about that while He was praying in a certain place, after he had finished, one of His disciples said to Him, Lord, teach us to pray just as John also taught his disciples. And He said to them, 'When you pray, say: Father, hallowed be Thy name. Thy kingdom come. Give us each day our daily bread and forgive our sins for we ourselves also forgive everyone who is indebted to us. And lead us not into temptation.'"

As devoted Jewish men, the disciples had grown up praying all of their lives. Yet something about the quality of Jesus' praying caused them to see how little they really knew about prayer. Jesus' prayer life was so compelling that his disciples were in awe. They wanted to learn how to pray as Jesus did. I find it highly significant that the disciples did not beg Jesus to teach them how to perform great miracles. They were moved most by Jesus' prayer life.

A disciple of Jesus will be like Him. And prayer is one distinctive mark of the follower of Jesus. When we put on the yoke of discipleship, we are led into the discipline of prayer.

Jesus' Prayer Life Was an Intimate Conversation

Jesus' prayer life was a foundational discipline that permeated his entire life and ministry, but it was more than a discipline—it was an intimate conversation. This is most evident in John 17. In what theologians describe as Jesus' high priestly prayer, we are given an intimate glimpse into Jesus' prayer life. I would encourage you to carefully read this chapter. Observe Jesus' transparency of heart. Notice the cooperation and love in the Triune Godhead by reading verses 24 through 26.

> *Father, I want those you have given me to be with me where I am, and to see my glory, the glory you have given me because you loved me before the creation of the world.*
>
> *Righteous Father, though the world does not know you, I know you, and they know that you have sent me.*
>
> *I have made you known to them, and will continue to make you known in order that the love you have for me may be in them and that I myself may be in them.*
>
> *John 17:24-26, NIV*

This is not some stuffy formal religious prayer—it is an incredible picture of an intimate conversation between two persons who are deeply in love with each other. If you listen closely, you can hear the beating of two divine hearts.

We must rethink our prayer paradigm. Often we think of prayer as talking to God. While this is an essential aspect of prayer, prayer is also listening to God. Soren Kierkegard once observed, "A man prayed, and at first he thought that prayer was talking, but he became more and more quiet until in the end he realized that prayer is listening."[vi] Prayer is a two-way conversation. Often we are not quiet enough or still long enough to hear God speak.

Learning to Listen

After many years of marriage, I have come to the humbling realization that I am severely romantically challenged. I think most men are born with a genetic predisposition to selective listening. Any wife who has ever tried to talk with her husband during a football game would verify the male gender's listening handicap. Thankfully, my bride of many years is patient and understanding, but I have had to learn a lot about what true intimacy is and how to experience it in a relationship between two sinful and fallen creatures.

One pearl of wisdom I have discovered in the crucible of marriage is that our intimacy is best when I listen most. Listening well requires hard work and great concentration. It also requires a quiet environment.

I believe what is true in marriage is also true in our relationship with God. The greatest lover of our soul woos us to a sacred romance where delicious spiritual intimacy awaits. But intimacy with God requires our embracing a posture of listening. Generally speaking, God will not compete for our attention. So often, our lives are just too preoccupied to hear God's voice.

We must not forget that God is, by His very nature, a communicative Being. John White in *Daring To Draw Near* makes this point, "God is always speaking. To hear his voice is not usually a mystical experience. It consists merely of a willingness to pay heed to the God who lays a claim on our lives...for the word 'hear' in the New Testament does not commonly refer to an auditory experience. More often it means 'to pay heed.' There's none so deaf...as them as won't hear."[vii]

God has revealed Himself to us through creation, through the Holy Scriptures and through Jesus the Incarnate Word. God's voice, whether through ordinary rational thought or an extraordinary mystical experience, is always consistent with His written word. In our discipline of prayer we must make time not only for speaking to God, but also for listening to Him speak to us.

Though prayer is an essential spiritual discipline, prayer was never meant to be a spiritual drudgery, but rather the soul's deepest delight. Prayer is an ongoing, intimate conversation with God about who we are and what we are doing together to build His kingdom. We enjoy no greater privilege than to develop intimacy with God. We find no greater friendship than the transforming personal relationship with Jesus Christ. William Law in his 18th century classic, *A Serious Call To A Devout And Holy Life,* said, "Prayer is the nearest approach to God and the highest enjoyment of him that we are capable of in this life."[viii] John Piper reminds us that God is most glorified when we are most satisfied in Him.

Although prayer is often a struggle, each of us should be

encouraged to realize that Jesus, in his incarnate being, modeled for us an awesome prayer life.

Where Do We Begin?

Prayer is a learning process. Because it is a process, we are set free to question, to experiment and even to fail. If you are just starting, don't be discouraged. Begin with just a few minutes a day. Like a muscle, prayer grows with use. Prayer, like any other discipline, grows with time and is encouraged by mentoring.

Read, learn, and memorize the prayers in Scripture. I suggest that you memorize a Psalm or two right away. You might also study and memorize part of Jesus' prayers or the Apostle Paul's prayers. One of my favorite prayers is found in Col. 1:9-11.

Our depth of prayer is related to how much our mind is soaked with Scriptural truth. The more we fill our minds with God's Word and the more we pray, the more we enjoy an intimate time with God. Another good way to learn the discipline of prayer is by studying the prayers of those in church history who have plumbed the depths of prayer. My mind has been enriched and my soul blessed by the writings of Andrew Murray, E. M. Bounds, and Henry Thornton. How then do we begin to grow in our prayer experience? I would suggest three specific steps.

Set a definite time and place

Seek out prayer mentors

Record your progress

Set A Definite Time & Place

The discipline of prayer demands our being intentional.

Carve out a regular time and a quiet place for prayer. Since we are all time-challenged, you will have to eliminate some good things in order to concentrate on the best things. Remember, a desire without a plan is only a dream. Both finding a quiet place and a regular time is essential if you are going to pick up the smooth stone of prayer.

Seek Prayer Mentors

Seek others who have a vibrant, growing prayer life and learn from them. After all, when we want to get into great physical shape, we seek a trainer to help us. Likewise, a trainer can help us in our spiritual disciplines. Find a spiritual mentor who will give you insight and accountability in your discipline of prayer. Look for individuals who seem to experience greater power and effectiveness in prayer than you do and ask them to teach you everything they know. Ask your small group leader or another leader in your church about being mentored in your prayer life. Ask these leaders what books on prayer have influenced them the most.

Record Your Progress

One of the most motivating aspects of my prayer life is to see how God has answered my prayers. Periodically, I record my prayers and prayer requests in a journal. Few things motivate me more in my discipline of prayer than seeing God answer prayers specifically. Record your journey. Begin keeping a prayer journal.

Remember the smooth stone of prayer, like all other disciplines, is a process. Begin where you are and move forward. He is waiting for you with outstretched arms.

Concluding Remarks

One of my most memorable lessons about prayer came from my daughter Sarah who was 11 months old. My prayer journal entry on that day read:

"On my way out of the house this morning, I crept quietly past Sarah's room not wanting to wake her. Yet as soon as I went by, she began to make her morning sounds. It seemed as if she was waiting for me.

"With such joy I went into her room. She was so excited to see me. With her outstretched arms she communicated that she wanted to be held. Her eyes sparkled and her smile widened.

"Almost instantly, the thought struck me, 'Oh, that I would approach my heavenly Father in the same way as Sarah does me. Truly, our heavenly Father must receive much joy when we, in devotion and dependence, desire fellowship with Him early in the morning.'"

Prayer is truly life's greatest privilege, the soul's greatest delight.

"Father, forgive us for the habit of tacking prayer onto the periphery of our lives. Father, meet us where we are and move us along into deeper things. Lord, teach us to pray! Make us a praying church! Grant us the grace to daily pick up the smooth stone of prayer."

With Christ In The School Of Prayer

And he taught them to pray:

Our Father, who art in heaven,
Hallowed be thy name.

Thy kingdom come.
Thy will be done on earth,
As it is in heaven.

Give us this day our daily bread.
And forgive us our trespasses,
As we forgive those who trespass against us.
And lead us not into temptation
But deliver us from evil:

For Thine is the kingdom,
And the power, and the glory,
Forever and ever.
Amen!

Questions

Evaluate Tom's assertion that "prayer is to the soul what oxygen is to the body."

What are three primary reasons Tom suggests that we struggle with prayer?

Which one of the three primary reasons can you relate to most? Why?

How did Jesus model an authentic and vibrant prayer life? (Give Scriptural support for your answer.)

Tom suggests that although prayer is a discipline, it is an intimate conversation with God. How does Jesus' prayer to the Father in John 17 communicate Jesus' intimacy with the Father?

How is prayer listening to God? What does effective listening require?

In the Sermon on the Mount, Jesus instructs His apprentices how to pray. What do you learn about prayer in Matthew 6:5-15?

Tom writes, "I believe our depth of prayer is related to the degree with which our mind is soaked with Scriptural truth." Do you agree? Why or why not?

What are some practical ways you can deepen your intimate conversation with God?

7

The Smooth Stone of Study

You shall love the Lord your God with all your heart and with all your soul and with all your mind. This is the great and first commandment. And a second is like it: You shall love your neighbor as yourself. Matthew 22:37-39

If I were to ask you what you feel is the greatest scandal of the contemporary evangelical church, what would you say?

Perhaps you would think of the scandalous downfall of the some ministry, or the moral meltdown of a prominent spiritual leader. Maybe you would mention the travesty of racism or the treachery of abortion. Perhaps you'd note the continued erosion of rampant materialism. Maybe you would question the church's indifference to the poor. Maybe your mind would dwell on some doctrinal error infiltrating the church.

As disturbing as all of these are, I do not believe they are the most scandalous. A more insidious scandal lurks beneath the shallow surface of our faith.

Mark Noll insightfully observes, "The scandal of the evangelical mind is that there is not much of an evangelical mind ... . Despite dynamic success at a popular level, modern American evangelicals have failed notably in sustaining serious intellectual life."[1]

A friend of mine who speaks to college students laments the wasteland of the mind in our universities. He describes, "Five percent of people think; 15 percent think they think; and 85 percent would rather die than think."

Tragically "I would rather die than think" is too often written on the tombstones of our intellectual graveyard.

We hear much about the revival of the heart—this is a needed and encouraging development. But why does such an eerie silence exist about the compelling need for a true renaissance of the Christian mind? Shouldn't we begin to address not only the lukewarmness of our hearts, but also the pervasive atrophy of our minds?

Many voices have warned us of the "dumbing down" of the church. A generation ago, P.T. Forsyth compellingly wrote, "There are few dangers threatening the religious future more serious than the slow shallowing of the religious mind ... . Our safety is in the deep. The lazy cry for simplicity is a great danger. It indicates a frame of mind which is only appalled at the great things of God, and a senility of faith which fears what is high."[ii]

Observing the flabby minds packing church pews in his day, Charles Malik, a Lebanese Christian, world statesmen, and former general secretary of the United Nations warned: "The greatest danger besetting American Evangelical Christianity is the danger of anti-intellectualism. The mind as to its greatness and deepest reaches is not cared for enough... . The problem is not only to win souls but to save minds."[iii]

The late A.W. Tozer put it this way: "Secularism, materialism, and the intrusive presence of things have put out the light in our souls, and turned us into a generation of zombies."

David Wells also warns the church of Jesus Christ. In *No Place for Truth,* he writes:

> A new species is now adrift in the world washing up all along the shores of evangelical life. It is a species eager to exchange enduring qualities for a spate of exciting new experiences, a species that thinks in terms of images rather than truths, that has no place from which to view the world but shifts from peephole to peephole in an attempt to catch the passing sights, a voyeur rather than a thinker, guided by a compass of circumstance, rather than belief.[IV]

As I survey the landscape of the contemporary church, the timeless words of the T.S. Eliot in his poem "The Hollow Men" ring with a melody of penetrating truth.

What is the greatest scandal inflicting the contemporary church? The greatest scandal is a shallow faith tenuously attached to personal feeling, instead of a deep faith tenaciously anchored to God's truth.

I love the story of Vince Lombardi, the legendary coach of the Green Bay Packers, who, after a humiliating defeat, gathered his team in the locker room. Exhorting them to get back to the basics, Lombardi picked up the pigskin, lifted it high in the air and said, "Men, this is a football."

Like Vince Lombardi, I often want to cry to the church, "People, this is God's Word." It is time for us to get back to the basics and seek to cultivate the mind!

Getting Back to Basics!

Contrary to His present-day church, Jesus viewed the mind's cultivation with great importance. We see this clearly in the

Great Commandment: "But when the Pharisees heard that He had put the Sadducees to silence, they gathered themselves together. And one of them, a lawyer, asked Him a question, testing Him, 'Teacher which is the great commandment in the Law?' And He said to him, 'You shall love the Lord your God with all your heart, and with all your soul and with all your mind. This is the great and foremost commandment. The second is like it, 'You shall love your neighbor as yourself. On these two commandments depend the whole Law and the prophets.'" (Matthew 22: 34-40)

In these seven verses, Jesus gets us back to the basics. Jesus was constantly challenged by the intelligent people of his day. In these challenges, Jesus demonstrated a truly astounding brilliance of mind. Matthew uses the same word in verse 34 as in verse 12 where it is translated "speechless." The apostle Paul also used this word in 1 Corinthians 9:9 to describe the muzzling of an ox.

The point made in verse 34 was that Jesus' mental capacity stunned the elite so that they were speechless. Intellectuals are known for many things, but not for their lack of words! Yet in this scripture, we see that the greatest minds of the day were stunned into silence by Jesus!

I don't know what comes into your mind when you think about Jesus, but one thing should be Jesus' extraordinary intellect. Jesus was intellectually in a class alone. Sometimes I think we quickly dismiss this and say, "Of course he had an awesome mind, after all He was the Son of God." But this misses the point, for Luke reminds us that Jesus grew in intellectual stature (Luke 2:52).

Responding to the question about the greatest commandment of the Old Testament, Jesus immediately recalled a text from the Old Testament Torah—a Torah He had studied rigorously as a child. In Matthew 22, Jesus quoted Deuteronomy 6:5, Moses' words of exhortation, "And you shall love the Lord your God with all your heart and with all your soul and with all your might."

Jesus added the word "mind" to that Old Testament text. Although heart, soul and mind overlap somewhat in their semantic range, mind carries a distinct meaning. The original word used here refers to one's intelligence—not just raw intelligence capacity, but also cerebral efficiency and clarity of thinking. Jesus' emphasis on the mind must have rubbed off on Peter, for Peter uses this same word when he exhorts the first century believers to holiness of living. Peter writes, "Therefore, gird your minds for action, keep sober in spirit, fix your hope completely on the grace to be brought to you at the revelation of Jesus Christ" (1 Peter 1:13).

What is Jesus' point in the Great Commandment? Undergirding a life well lived is a God well loved. A God well loved must be a God well known. To love someone deeply we must seek to know that person intimately. This makes sense because you cannot truly love someone deeply until you know him or her intimately. This requires not only being involved in the person's life, but also cognitively understanding him or her.

Loving God intimately is not only an experiential journey of the heart but also a journey of the mind. As Jesus' apprentices, we are called to vigorously engage in the life of the mind.

A.W. Tozer said, "What comes into our minds when we think about God is the most important thing about us. The history of mankind will probably show that no people has ever risen above its religion, and man's spiritual history will positively demonstrate that no religion has ever been greater than its idea of God. Worship is pure or base as the worshiper entertains high or low thoughts of God."[v]

A Personal Note

Liz and I have been married for almost 20 years. Before we were married we sought premarital counseling and went to a marriage conference together. We read books on marriage and listened to people's advice. One piece of advice has stayed riveted to me: "Never stop being a student of your spouse." I don't always succeed in this discipline, but I have continually attempted to learn more about Liz in our years of marriage.

And as I learn more about her, I am able to love her more and meet her needs better. When you really love someone, you study him or her. Not only is your heart attached to that person, but your mind is focused on him or her.

This is particularly true in loving God. We must understand that feelings are vital, but not foundational.

In *Cries Of The Heart,* Ravi Zacharias says, "Nothing is so important to the nature of a word as the truth, and truth is the property of propositions not feelings. Feelings are never described as true or false. Feelings may be legitimate or illegitimate, understandable or incomprehensible, but they are not true or false. This is where we get bogged down, longing for feelings, when indeed those very feelings could be the most seductive force to take us away from the truth."[vi]

So often we build our lives on our feelings rather than on truth. The phrase in the song, "You Light Up My Life," that say "It can't be wrong, if it feels so right," seem to be our ethical mantra. Jesus commands us to love Him not only with our heart and soul, but with our mind as well. Loving God with our minds is vital in our worship of Him. Thoughts and ideas about God that are not worthy of Him, that do not correspond to the revelation of Holy Scripture, are the most grotesque form of idolatry. In the great commandment Jesus exhorts each one of us to love God with all of our minds, but what does this mean?

What Does It Mean to Love God with Our Minds?

First of all, loving God with our minds does not mean Christianity is just for the intellectual. Loving God with our minds does not demand that we have a certain level of formal education. Jesus honored child-like faith, but I cannot find any place in scripture in which He honored ignorant, weak, or undisciplined minds.

We must remember the hideous monster of pride often lurks in the shadows of intellectual pursuit; yet we must also remember that pride injects its poisonous venom in the flesh of ignorance. Ignorance is Satan's handmaiden, not the ally of authentic faith. An undisciplined mind is fertile ground for deception. The character, Professor Harold Hill, in that famous musical "The Music Man," says it well: "The idol brain is the devil's playground." Paul shares these thoughts:

But I am fearful, lest that even as the serpent beguiled Eve by his cunning, so your minds may be corrupted and seduced from wholehearted and sincere and pure devotion to Christ. 2 Corinthians 11:3

In his 18th century classic, *A Serious Call To A Devout And Holy Life,* William Law writes: "Devotion, therefore, is so far from being best suited to little ignorant minds that a true elevation of soul, a lively sense of honor, and a great knowledge of God and ourselves are the greatest natural helps for our devotion. It shall now be made to appear by a variety of arguments that indevotion (or lack of devotion to God) is founded on the most excessive ignorance."[vii]

We often glibly say, "Ignorance is bliss." But actually, ignorance of God and His word is anything but bliss—it is tragic and often leads to death. Christianity is not a mindless faith; it is a mindful faith. Christianity, unlike New Age religion, is not an emptying of the mind, but rather an engaging of the mind. Authentic Christianity not only transforms the heart; but also transforms the mind. Romans 12:2 instructs, "Do not be conformed to this world, but be transformed by the renewing of your minds."

What does it mean to love God with our minds? I believe it involves two foundational building blocks. We must cultivate a devotion to the Holy Scripture and embrace the discipline of study.

Cultivate a Devotion to Holy Scripture!

When we love God, we love His Word. Jesus said, "If you abide in My word, then you are truly disciples of mine, and you shall know the truth and the truth shall set you free." (John 8:31-32)

The Apostle Paul passionately exhorted believers in Colossae, "Let the word of Christ richly dwell within you ... . " (Col. 3:16). In Acts, Luke commended the believers in Berea, "Now these were more noble-minded than those in Thessalonica, for they received the word with great eagerness, examining the Scriptures daily to see whether things were so" (Acts 17:11).

As a new generation of God's people were about to enter the promised land, God exhorted Joshua to keep the Word of God anchored to his life and leadership: "This book of the law shall not depart from your mouth, but you shall meditate on it day and night, so that you may be careful to do according to all that is written in it, for then you will make your way prosperous, and then you will have success" (Joshua 1:8).

The Psalms emphasize the importance of the believers' devotion to Scripture. Psalm 119 contains 176 verses dedicated to the importance of devoting our minds and hearts on Scripture.

In verse 162, the Psalmist declares, "I rejoice at Thy word as one who finds great spoil." In our culture, we might translate this "I rejoice in God's Word like one who wins the powerball lottery." The word of God is like a great treasure. It holds transforming truth waiting for all who will dig for it.

Jesus said, "The kingdom of heaven is like a treasure hidden in the field which a man found and hid, and from joy over it he goes and sells all that he has to buy that field" (Matthew 13:44). The treasure of the kingdom of heaven is found in the field of God's Word. As we seek this treasure our priorities are altered and our passions are transformed. When we love God with our minds, we devote ourselves to the Scriptures. God's Word is the original version of *Chicken Soup for the Soul!*

We are called to be people of the Holy Book—people whose minds are saturated with scriptural truth!

I love the story former missionary Elisabeth Elliot tells about visiting Corrie ten Boom. Corrie ten Boom had endured great suffering at the Nazis' hands during World War II. She landed in a prison camp for helping Jewish people hide. Elisabeth said that during their delightful conversation she asked Corrie how we should prepare for suffering. Corrie emphatically responded, "Soak in the Word!"[viii]

Embrace the Discipline of Study

Soaking in God's Word does not happen by osmosis—it requires discipline of mind. Again, we must remember that although grace is opposed to merit, it is not opposed to effort. Divine enablement and human cooperation are both essential in being a disciple of Jesus Christ.

When we love God with all our of minds we exert effort and embrace the discipline of study. Dietrich Bonhoeffer adamantly declared, "One who will not learn to handle the Bible for himself is not an evangelical Christian."[ix]

I believe the discipline of study is the second foundational imperative to those who want to passionately pursue a great love for Almighty God. The discipline of study is simply letting our minds absorb the reality of God. The discipline of study is primarily focused on the Scriptures.

Although the New Testament does not explicitly describe the many hours Jesus studied, the results of His lifestyle discipline are overwhelmingly evident. Although we are given little information concerning Jesus' early life, Luke does gives us a brief glimpse of Jesus as a young boy. What do we see? Jesus was found by his frantic earthly parents after three days of being lost. Where do they find Him? He was talking with Jerusalem's religious leaders about the truths of Scripture (Luke 2:46-47). Jesus' mastery of the Old Testament scriptures was unmatched. This is evidence not only of his divine mind, but also his disciplined human mind. We are tempted to think that because Jesus was God's Son he didn't have to embrace the discipline of study, but this is faulty thinking. Jesus, as the Son of God, engaged in other spiritual disciplines of prayer, fasting and solitude. Jesus modeled in His incarnate state one who loved God the Father with His mind. His life and ministry are irrefutable evidence of His discipline of study.

In making the Great Commandment a cornerstone of His teaching, Jesus influenced not only Judaism, but also the early church. To love God with not only one's heart and soul, but also with one's mind was a central aspect of authentic Christian discipleship in the early church.

What has happened to this vital commitment for those of us who profess to follow Jesus Christ and live in the postmodern age? How often are we more concerned with physically conditioning our bodies than intellectually conditioning our minds? We often spend much more time each week in workout rooms than in our quiet places of study, memorization, and reading. Flabby bodies are one thing; flabby minds are quite another!

In 1 Timothy, Paul urges his disciple, Timothy, "Discipline yourself for the purpose of godliness, for bodily discipline is only of little profit, but godliness is profitable for all things ... ." Shortly before he was martyred in Rome, Paul reminded Timothy of the importance of the spiritual discipline, especially the discipline of study, "Study to show yourself approved unto God, as a workman who does not need to be ashamed, handling accurately the word of truth" (2 Timothy 2:15).

Paul reminded Timothy that he must discipline himself in study to be "approved unto God." The discipline of study is fueled by a burning passion for truth and a fervent love for Almighty God. When we love God with our minds, we embrace the discipline of study. Our hearts cannot deeply love what our minds do not truly know.

Like the smooth stone of solitude and the smooth stone of prayer, we must weave the discipline of study into the fabric of our lives.

Where do we begin? Let me suggest four action points.

Embark on a Disciplined Regimen of Bible Study

Watch out for *The Daily Bread* syndrome! Devotionals like *The Daily Bread* are wonderful, but are not a substitute for regular study of God's Word. Also watch out for the Sunday Morning Sermon syndrome! Tragically, many followers of Jesus rely on a Sunday morning sermon to feed their souls and invigorate their minds for the entire week. No sermon, no matter how well crafted and passionately delivered, can take the place of personal Bible study. Sermons are meant to prime the pump for us so that we go to the well of truth during the week.

No matter where we are in our spiritual journey, each of us needs a regular disciplined study of the Bible. We need to read the entire Scriptures through repeatedly. We must get the big picture of God's revelation and observe the wonder of His redemptive story. Reading Bible guides and Walk Thru The Bible materials are helpful for this. We also need analytical Bible study, through which we learn how to study the Bible in detail. Inductive Bible studies like Precepts, Community Bible Study, and Bible Study Fellowship are wonderful tools to move us further down the path to effective personal Bible study.

Bible study is a skill that needs to be learned and requires discipline and effort. Yet great rewards await those who will seek its inexhaustible treasures!

Eliminate Mental Junk Food From Your Diet

In this postmodern age our lives are stuffed with information, as never before, yet our souls reveal an acute starvation from the lack of God's truth. When we do read, we often fill our minds with mental junk food. Not all books are equally nourishing to the mind. In many ways, we are what we put into our minds.

Read the Scriptures with your family. Read Bill Bennett's *Book of Virtues* and *The Moral Compass*. Develop a reading list of Christian classics and begin a program to read through them. Few things are more mind-numbing than excessively viewing TV and video games. Loving God with all of our hearts, souls, and minds is something that is not only taught, but also caught, by our children. Make your home a place where young minds are nourished and challenged—a place where great ideas dwell! Don't let your children's minds, or your own mind, be malnourished with mental junk food.

Engage In A Regular Scripture Memorization Program

I recommend that you use the Navigator's topical memory system to imbed God's Word into your mind. Memorize Scripture with your children. And don't just find easy verses, memorize large sections of scripture like 1 Cor. 13, Phil. 2, and Ps. 1. Join a small group in which you can be accountable to others for Scripture memory. Listen to tapes of Scripture in your car and home. Learn and sings songs laced with Scripture texts. One blessing of contemporary Christian music is that many of the lyrics come directly from God's Word.

Embrace the Spiritual Masters

Those who have gone before us have much to teach us. The Christian church over the centuries has included a treasure of brilliant minds and devoted hearts. Some of our most important mentors are godly men and women who lived long ago. Men and women who have been yoked with Jesus Christ have left treasures for us to glean through their timeless writings. Follow the path others have blazed! "Remember those who led you, who spoke the word of God to you; and considering the result of their conduct, imitate their faith" (Hebrews 13:7).

The words of 17th century philosopher Blaise Pascal still ring with astounding clarity, "Truth is so obscured nowadays and lies so well established that unless we love the truth we shall never recognize it."[x] We must cultivate a love for truth! To cultivating this love for truth, it is helpful to engage in the great conversation of the church throughout the centuries.

Avoiding Two Perilous Myths

In our finitude and fallenness, we must humbly admit we do not have all the answers. God's Word is an awesome treasure, but does not reveal all of the answers to our seemingly infinite specific questions. But just because we do not have all the answers does not mean we have no answers. Not having all truth does not mean we have no truth. This is a fallacy of much contemporary thinking that often makes the pursuit of truth a mere subjective whim. Our contemporary culture abhors dogmatism, choosing instead to embrace more mystery and paradox!

In our passionate pursuit of truth, we must be aware of two myths that threaten to sidetrack our spiritual journey. We must avoid the myth of certainty and the myth of sincerity.

The myth of certainty creates an illusion of absolute knowing that only God Himself possesses. Clinging to the myth of certainty is a precarious perch for any finite creature because those who do so often find themselves in the quagmire of proud dogmatism.

On the other end of the knowledge continuum, the myth of sincerity declares that truth is merely whatever I sincerely believe! The myth of sincerity places all truth claims within the subjective musings of a fallen and finite creature. Those who embrace the myth of sincerity slide down a slippery slope of confusion and will lose all truth.

In a satirical poem, "Creed," Steve Turner penetrates the absurdity of the myth of sincerity. "We believe that each man must find the truth that is right for him. Reality will adapt accordingly. The universe will readjust. History will alter. We believe there is not absolute truth excepting the truth that there is no absolute truth."[xi]

Both myths usurp the boundaries of the created and place us in God the Creator's exclusive domain. By clinging to either myth, we play God and display our proud arrogance! Both myths extinguish the sense of wonder—the wonder due to our infinite and awesome God. The smooth stone of study should lead us to an ever-increasing sense of wonder and worship before a Holy and Righteous Heavenly Father. At times the answers we want will evade us, but a sense of awe will greet us. Our God is an amazing God!

Concluding Remarks

Few people today have walked closer to God or been used by God in a greater way than Billy Graham. On November 15,

1993, *Time* magazine gave tribute to Billy Graham. Much in the article that warmed my heart and fueled my passion, but I also found prophetic words of warning from this extraordinary man of God. Reflecting on his life, Billy Graham describes his one great regret. Graham confided, "I had one great failure, and that was intellectual. I should have gone on to school. But I would talk to people about that, and they'd say. 'Oh no, go on with what you are doing, and let others do that.' I do regret I didn't do enough reading, enough study, both formal and informal."[xii]

We must pick up the smooth stone of study, for our hearts cannot deeply love what our minds do not truly know.

> *"But an hour is coming, and now is, when the true worshipers will worship the Father in spirit and truth; for such people the Father seeks to be His worshipers. God is spirit, and those who worship Him must worship in spirit and truth." John 4:23-24*

> *Teach us Lord to worship you in spirit and truth.*
> *Amen and amen!*

Questions

What is the "scandal of the evangelical mind?"

How does Tom assess the current state of the Evangelical church when it comes to the life of the mind? Do you agree? Why or why not?

How do we see Jesus emphasizing the importance of the cultivation of the mind? (Give Scriptural support for your answers.)

How did Jesus demonstrate his intellectual capacity and brilliance?

What does Tom mean when he states, "Loving God rightly is not only an experiential journey of the heart, but also a cerebral journey of the mind?"

What does it mean to love God with our minds?

What is the relationship between loving God with our minds and becoming students of Holy Scripture?

Comment on Tom's assertion, "Our hearts cannot deeply love what our minds do not truly know."

What does Tom mean by "eliminating mental junk food from your diet?"

What are some practical ways you can pick up the smooth stone of study?

8

The Smooth Stone of Fasting

But you, when you fast, anoint your head and wash your face so that you may not be seen fasting by men, but by your father who is in secret, and your Father who sees in secret will reward you. Matthew 6:17-18

Wrestlers think about few things more than they dream of food. As a teenager whose passion was wrestling, I was no exception. One stark reality which hangs over the head of every wrestler is "making weight," except the heavy weight class, of course. In our machismo we dismissed the heavyweights as soft, but most of us faced an ominous reality that if we didn't weigh the right amount, we didn't wrestle. No excuses! No exceptions!

Staying at our natural weight was not an option if we wanted to be competitive, so we all had to drop weight and go down to a lower weight class. To this day, I still recall the agony of watching television commercials of fast-food chains. Pizzas loaded with cheese, sausage and mushrooms, and juicy hamburgers with all the works tormented me. I salivated like Pavlov's dog. The absolute killer was missing the Thanksgiving meal because of an early season tournament the following week. I also discovered that all of my social interaction with family and friends was centered around food. One of my wrestling buddies felt so deprived he had his parents put his Thanksgiving dinner and every dessert that he missed during the season in a large freezer. When the season was over, he planned to eat all he had missed. Somehow the anticipation of this future reward helped him be more disciplined.

I will spare you the gory details of how I cut weight to improve my competitive edge, but a lasting lesson emerged from my extreme and, at times, unwise competitive obsession. My regular fasting made me realize just how much my life and our entire culture is centered around food. Food is so ingrained in our way of living that even the thought of going without a meal, or several meals, seems foreign to our way of thinking.

Richard Foster in *Celebration of Discpline,* begins a chapter on the discipline of fasting with these insightful words: "In a culture where the landscape is dotted with shrines to the Golden Arches and an assortment of Pizza Temples, fasting seems out of place, out of step with the times."[i]

For many, the idea of fasting may seem a bit out of sync with the times, yet all around us is a growing spiritual interest in fasting.

In an article from the *Kansas City Star,* "Finding Spirituality On A Path Of Fasting," writer Eric Adler noted, "In recent years interest in fasting as a personal way to become closer to God and as a collective way to heal what some see as the country's considerable moral wounds—has been burgeoning nationwide."[ii]

What are we to make of this growing interest in fasting?

Despite the danger of being caught in a deceptive spiritual fad boldly promoted by spiritual gurus, this renewed interest in fasting is generally an encouraging development. The Holy

Scriptures and the long tradition of the church of Jesus Christ bear strong witness of fasting's timeless importance to those who would follow Jesus in His yoke of discipleship. Arthur Wallis in *God's Chosen Fast*, writes:

> For nearly a century and a half fasting has been out of vogue, at least in the churches of the West. The very idea of someone actually fasting today seems strange to most twentieth-century Christians. They associate it with medieval Christianity, or perhaps High Church practices. They may recall that political leaders, like Mahatma Gandhi, have used it as a weapon of passive resistance. As a spiritual exercise it is confined, they would think, to believers who appear to be a little extreme or fanatical.[iii]

Fasting has been abused as a leverage for political power or as a legalistic self-righteous means to an empty external religion. Fasting has also been hailed as a miraculous cure. Exaggerated claims of the physical benefits from fasting have been fertile ground for health quackery.

The abuse of fasting is well documented in many world religions and yes, in the history of the Christian church, especially during the Middle Ages. A Platonic dualism infiltrated the church that held the idea that the body was evil and only the immaterial aspect of mankind was good. This false view of the body led to physical abuses. Unbalanced views of fasting were often the culprit of asceticism.

Although fasting has been abused in church history, it has also been neglected. For many Christ-followers, fasting has been removed not only from the periphery of Christian experience, but it has been moved to the remote edge of historical curiosity. John Wesley, founder of the Methodist church, summarized the church's volatile experience with fasting this way: "Some have exalted religious fasting beyond all reason; others have utterly disregarded it."[iv]

In our contemporary culture with its growing longing for a deeper spirituality, the flag of fasting is being waved with renewed enthusiasm. Prayer and fasting conferences are being organized. More books are addressing the subject. This fasting renaissance includes the heralding of many spiritual and physical benefits of fasting. This cacophony of voices brings an abundance of emotional sentiment and a disturbing lack of true biblical reflection.

In addressing the spiritual discipline of fasting, I admit I feel a bit torn, like Frank Symanski, the Notre Dame center in the 1940s. Frank had been called as a witness in a civil suit at South Bend. After putting his hand on a Bible and swearing to tell the whole truth and nothing but the truth, the judge engaged him in a brief conversation:

> "Are you on the Notre Dame football team this year?"
> "Yes, Your Honor," Frank replied.
> "What is your position?"
> "Center, Your Honor."
> "How good a center?"
> Frank Symanski squirmed in his seat, but said firmly, "Sir, I'm the best center Notre Dame has ever had."
> Coach Frank Leahy, who was in the courtroom, was surprised. Frank Symanski always had been modest and unassuming. So when the proceedings were over, he took Frank Symanski aside and asked why he had made such a statement. Frank blushed. "I hated to do it, Coach," he said. "But, after all, I was under oath."[v]

As a pastor, I feel the importance of the stewardship I have been given to teach the whole counsel of God. In a sense I am "under oath" before my Audience of One. Yet I realize that though fasting is a part of that whole counsel, it often leads well-meaning people off in some dangerous tangent or piles them under a load of false guilt. I pray that you will avoid both of these soul-suffocating perils.

The Bible speaks considerably on fasting. Fasting is referred to over seventy times in the Old Testament and over thirty five times in the New Testament. In addressing fasting, I would like to raise two important questions for our consideration.

How Did Jesus View Fasting?

Jesus Embraced Fasting

In Matt. 4:1-4 we read, "Then Jesus was led up by the Spirit into the wilderness to be tempted by the devil. And after He had fasted forty days and forty nights, He then became hungry. And the tempter came and said to Him, 'If you are the Son of God, command that these stones become bread.' But He answered and said, 'It is written, Man shall not live on bread alone, but on every word that proceeds out of the mouth of God.'"

The text is explicit, leaving little room for us to doubt that Jesus fasted. Although this was a highly unusual fast in that it lasted forty days, this text gives us insight into Jesus' understanding of fasting. The Holy Spirit, like a trainer of a prizefighter, whisked Jesus away into the wilderness for special spiritual training. Fasting was an essential aspect of that training. Fasting did not weaken Jesus, but strengthened and prepared Him for His encounter with Satan.

Notice that the Evil One tempted Jesus first at a bodily level. He tempted Jesus to satisfy His body's desire for food. Why? Dr. Neil Anderson observes, "Eating is the granddaddy of all appetites. Fasting is a commitment to bring about self-control and overcome every other conceivable temptation."[vi]

Satan told Jesus, "If you are the Son of God, command that these stones become bread." Now observe that Jesus answered Satan by quoting Deuteronomy 8:3, "But He answered and said, 'Man shall not live on bread alone, but on every word that proceeds out of the mouth of God.'"

Jesus' statement from the Old Testament was important. Jesus reinforced a foundational truth that humans are much more than their physical bodies. Jesus emphasized the spiritual nature and essence of mankind. We are not mere physical bodies. We are never ceasing spiritual beings with an eternal destiny in God's great universe. Our primary essence is not that of a physical consumer, but that of a spiritual worshipper of the living, eternal God.

In a consumerist culture, we tend to define ourselves in terms of what we have and do, rather than who we are. Our idolatrous framework is one of having, rather than one of being. The subtle snare of materialism has slowly and imperceptibly squeezed its soul-suffocating noose around our lives.

Jesus reminded us we were made to be eternal worshippers, not merely temporal consumers. Our spiritual being is nourished, strengthened, and sustained not by physical food, but by God's Word. When we fast from physical food, we feast on God's Word. Fasting is feasting; feasting our inner being on God. In fasting, our spiritual being is nourished and strengthened.

When we fast, our hunger that is often directed toward food is directed toward God. In fasting we reinforce the reality that our physical body is not to be our master, but our servant. Dallas Willard writes, "Fasting confirms our utter dependence upon God by finding in him a source of sustenance beyond food. Through it, we learn by experience that God's word to us is a life substance, that it is not food (bread) alone that gives life, but also the words that proceed from the mouth of God ... . Fasting unto our Lord is, therefore, feasting—feasting on him and on doing His will."[vii]

A Biblical Illustration

Like us, Jesus' disciples, who were locked into three square meals a day, had a hard time understanding spiritual nourishment. In John 4 we see the account of Jesus ministering to the Samaritan woman at the well. The disciples had gone into town to get some food. When they came back, they urged Jesus to eat. Notice Jesus' response, "I have food to eat that you do not know about."

The disciples were perplexed. They wondered how Jesus got food when they were gone. Jesus then said, "My food is to do the will of Him who sent Me and to accomplish His work" (John 4:32,34). I get the sense that after this dialogue, the disciples were still scratching their heads in bewilderment. Like us, they missed what Jesus was trying to say.

Jesus Endorsed Fasting.

In the Sermon on the Mount, Jesus not only endorsed fasting, but also emphasized the importance of proper motives when fasting:

> *And whenever you fast, do not put on a gloomy face as the hypocrites do, for they neglect their appearance in order to be seen fasting by men.*

Truly I say to you, they have their reward in full. But you, when you fast, anoint your head and wash your face so that you may not be seen fasting by men, but by your father who is in secret, and your Father who sees in secret will reward you. Matthew 6:16-18

Jesus anticipated that his disciples would fast. In Matt. 9, we read that John the Baptist's disciples asked Jesus why his disciples did not fast. In verse 15, Jesus said, "The attendants of the bridegroom cannot mourn as long as the bridegroom is with them, can they? But the days will come when the bridegroom is taken away from them, and then they will fast."

John Piper in his excellent book on fasting, *A Hunger For God,* captures the essence of fasting. "Fasting is a physical expression of heart-hunger for the coming of Jesus... . Therefore, one of the most important meanings of Christian fasting is to express the hunger of our hearts for the coming of our King."viii

We need to remember that to be a disciple of Jesus, we must not only embrace His teachings, but also His practices. As His disciple, I am learning to live like Jesus would if He were me. Jesus practiced the discipline of fasting. Like Jesus we are also called to practice the spiritual discipline of fasting. We must not abuse or neglect this important spiritual discipline.

What Are the Delights and Dangers of Fasting?

Through the inspired pen of Isaiah, we find one of the most definitive texts on fasting in the Scriptures:

Why have we fasted, they say, and you have not seen it? Why have we humbled ourselves, and you have not noticed? Yet on the day of your fasting, you do as you please

and exploit your workers. Your fasting ends in quarreling and strife, and in striking each other with wicked fists. You cannot fast as you do today and expect your voice to be heard on high. Is this the kind of fast I have chosen, only a day for a man to humble himself? Is it only for bowing one's head like a reed and for lying on sackcloth and ashes? Is this what you call a fast, a day acceptable to the Lord? Is not the kind of fasting I have chosen: to loose the chains of injustice and untie the cords of the yoke, to set the oppressed free and break every yoke? Is it not to share your food with the hungry and to provide the poor wanderer with shelter–when you see the naked, to clothe him and not to turn away from your own flesh and blood? Then your light will break forth like the dawn, and your healing will quickly appear; then your righteousness will go before you, and the glory of the Lord will be your rear guard. Then you will call, and the Lord will answer; you will cry for help, and will say: Here am I. If you do away with the yoke of oppression, with the pointing of the finger and malicious talk, and if you spend yourselves in behalf of the hungry and satisfy the needs of the oppressed, then your light will rise in darkness, and your night will become like noonday. The Lord will guide you always; he will satisfy your needs in a sun-scorched land and will strengthen your frame. You will be like a well-watered garden, like a spring whose waters never fail.

Isa. 58:3-11, NIV

In this extraordinary passage of rich metaphorical images, Isaiah paints a compelling and contrasting portrait of enslavement and intimacy, of burden and blessing. This is a portrait painted on the canvass of fasting. In this portrait, I see two primary dangers in fasting.

Two Primary Dangers of Fasting

Fasting May Become a Religious Rabbit's Foot

In verse three, God's people complained that they had gone through the motions of fasting, but God had not noticed. In other words, they were fasting in order to get something from God, rather than fasting to get to know God. T.S. Eliot once observed, "The greatest treason is to do the right thing for the wrong reason." This is a subtle danger we must avoid as we approach this discipline. We do not fast to merit anything before God or to obligate Him to act according to our wishes. Our fasting does not place God under some sort of divine obligation to answer our prayer or to bring revival to our nation. Fasting is not a rabbit's foot to get God to act or intervene in a way we feel He should.

Fasting May Become a Ritualistic Form.

In verses three to five, Isaiah described the spiritual hypocrisy of God's people. They abstained from food, but engaged in personal vice and the oppression of others. In other words they were going through religious motions, but their inner lives were not changed. True fasting leads to a transformation of the heart. It also leads to a transformation of how we deal with others. We must be careful lest a fasting fad becomes an external religious conformity and not an authentic quest to know God more intimately.

While in the Middle East, I observed many of the religious practices not only of Christians and Jews, but also of Muslims.

My wife and I were in Jordan during the Muslim holiday Ramadan. During Ramadan, faithful Muslims fast for several days from sunup to sundown. Having ridden in taxis and buses during Ramadan, I must tell you it creates a very irritable population. But I soon discovered from Muslim friends that they get around the system by feasting at night. So not only are they hungry during the day, they are exhausted from staying up late at night catching up on their caloric intake. I am sure some devout Muslims see the call to fasting during Ramadan as a meaningful spiritual experience, but many go through the external motions of fasting, while their thoughts flee far from anything spiritual. Fasting during Ramadan was for many of them a mere cultural drudgery.

But from a biblical perspective, fasting is to embrace spiritual delight. I see in Isaiah two primary delights of fasting.

Two Primary Delights of Fasting

Fasting Shatters the Shackles of Enslavement

The repeated metaphor in verses 6 through 11 is the yoke. Unlike the easy yoke of Christ, this yoke carries personal enslavement to sin, and the societal injustice and oppression of others. In verse 6, Isaiah painted a vivid picture that fasting loosens the grip on those things that enslave us as well as society.

Isaiah used powerful imagery to reveal how fasting breaks the shackles of things that enslave us. In verse 5, Isaiah addresses the enslavement of the pride of our hearts. King David refers to fasting's power to humble our souls. The Psalmist declared, "I humbled my soul with fasting" (Psalm 35:13). Fasting chisels away the barnacles of pride that cling to our hearts.

For two years I served college students at the University of Kansas through the ministry of Campus Crusade for Christ. Facing obstacle after obstacle and seeing little spiritual fruit, our ministry staff team chose to fast and pray for three days. In those three days God began to work in the lives of the staff, chipping away our pride and moving us to a desperate dependence on Him. Although we did not know it then, God was preparing the way for some of the most fruitful ministry years ever seen on the Kansas University campus.

Today, we look back on our three days of fasting and prayer as a turning point in the ministry. Many students came to faith in Christ and are serving Him all around the world. God desired to do some major "heart" surgery in order for us to be usable for His kingdom. Our obedience to fasting and prayer made room for God to do a necessary work in our lives. The greatest ministry obstacle was not out "there" somewhere, but in our own hearts.

In verse 6, Isaiah addressed the enslavement of power in our hearts. Our enslavement to the tentacles of power is seen in the dispensation of societal justice. Fasting breaks the shackles of the abuse of power and oppression. Fasting releases the smothering grip of fatal conceit on our hearts.

I have heard this text heralded as a reference to spiritual warfare, with fasting empowering us to conquer the Evil One. Although other scriptures *might* support this concept, this text clearly does not—either linguistically or contextually. Isaiah is not primarily talking about our wrestling with spiritual entities; he is talking about our relationship with others in society. We should not be surprised at this for societal justice is near to God's heart. Micah, a contemporary prophet of Isaiah, declares, "He has told you, O man, what is good, and what does the Lord require of you, but to do justice, love kindness and walk humbly with your God" (Micah 6:8). Fasting not only breaks the shackles of pride and power, it also breaks the shackles of self-absorption and greed. Isaiah reminds us of this in verse 7. Fasting removes us from preoccupation with self and our material things and sensitizes us to the needs of others, the hungry, the homeless, and the naked. Bill Bright reinforces this idea, "Fasting reduces the power of self so that the Holy Spirit can do a more intense work within us."[ix]

When we are unshackled from the fleshly enslavements to pride, power, greed and self-absorption, we are free to enjoy a more intimate relationship with God.

Fasting Enhances Intimacy With God

In verse 8, Isaiah described a result of fasting: "Then your light will break out like the dawn, and your recovery will speedily spring forth, and your righteousness will go before you, the glory of the Lord will be your rear guard."

Isaiah's vivid imagery points to a spiritual awakening, a newness of life, a wholeness of soul. In verse 9, Isaiah emphasized a new intimacy with God that results from fasting—a more satisfying relationship to God, a closer sense of His presence and answers to prayer. "Then you will call and the Lord will answer, You will cry, and He will say, Here I am."

When we embrace the discipline of fasting, we are also endowed with greater spiritual vision and power. In verse 10, Isaiah described a light rising in darkness, an image of spiritual vision, hope and influence. In verse 11, Isaiah declared, "And the Lord will continually guide you, and satisfy your desire (soul) in scorched places, and give strength to your bones; and you will be like a watered garden, and like a spring of water whose waters do not fail."

Isaiah was saying that the discipline of fasting produces an overflowing inner life, a purity of heart, and a wholeness of soul.

Patches of Godlight on the Washington Mall

On October 4, 1997, more than one million men gathered on the Washington Mall for a sacred assembly. I, along with many men from the church I serve, flew to Washington D.C. to be a part of this historic event. With the calling of the ancient shofar a million men hit their knees seeking God. It was a moment I will always cherish, a moment impossible to explain. A taste of heaven perhaps! Radiant patches of Godlight to be sure! The fresh breezes of eternity invigorated our souls.

The planners of this massive gathering had gone to great lengths to provide a million meals for the participants, but something amazing happened. The men had come to Washington D.C. with a gnawing hunger for God, not for food. Many men were fasting and the organizers faced a new problem: What could they to do with a million meals? The solution was simple: feed the poor and hungry of Washington D.C. Eighteen-wheeler after eighteen-wheeler moved from the mall to the city, delivering nutritious meals to homeless shelters and food pantries.

On that day we received a double portion of joy—the joy of seeking God and the joy of caring for others!

Tragically, we have neglected the discipline of fasting and have, therefore, missed out on some great joy. This neglect has also contributed to the shallow, anemic state of our hearts as well as to our encumbered souls. God's Word reminds us that fasting breaks the shackles that enslave us. Fasting deepens our intimacy with God. Fasting endows us with spiritual vision and power. The discipline of fasting is an important part of following in Jesus' footsteps.

How Do We Get Started?

Do a Bible Study on Fasting

Using a Bible concordance, look up the verses that contain the word fasting. Examine what the Bible says. You will notice different kinds of fasts, but each has a distinct spiritual purpose. Keep in mind that fasting is not starving the body, it is feeding the spirit. Maintain the proper motives and the proper purpose in mind when you fast. Fasting is not for the spiritual elite; it is a spiritual discipline for all apprentices who want to put on Jesus' yoke of discipleship.

Read a Good Book on Fasting

Be discerning in what you read. A lot of nuts reside among the berries! Richard Foster's, *Celebration of Discipline* and Dallas Willard's, *The Spirit Of The Disciplines,* both have good sections on fasting. Another good book is *A Hunger For God* by John Piper. All three of these authors blend good biblical and philosophical reflection with practical insight.

Begin the Discipline of Fasting Wisely

For many of us, considering fasting is a new idea. Like any other discipline, start where you are and take small steps forward. Begin by skipping a meal and use that time to pray and read the Bible. Perhaps you are hungering for a deeper relationship with Christ. Maybe you are enduring a difficult time. Perhaps you need guidance concerning a decision you are facing.

Take an extended time, an afternoon, a day, or a weekend to fast and pray. Ask another Christian who practices the discipline of fasting for help and guidance.

Before you fast, consult a physician if you have a medical condition. Fasting can injure the health of some people with medical conditions. I do not advise fasting for children or teenagers.

Stay Balanced

Guard against extremes. Solomon reminds us of the importance of balance in our lives. In Ecclesiastes 7:16, Solomon exhorts, "Do not be excessively righteous... ."

Some of us have the tendency to jump on the latest spiritual bandwagon and ride it with reckless abandon until we hit the wall of burnout and disillusionment. Don't do an extended fast (such as more than two or three days) without experience, direction from the Lord, and wise counsel.

Fasting is not to be abused or neglected. Stay balanced as you walk in the power of the Holy Spirit.

Closing Thoughts

Mike Yaconelli describes his enlightening journey into wholeness of soul on the path of the spiritual disciplines, "It only took a few hours of silence to realize I had become a stranger to myself ... . I recognized that the rugged terrain of my soul was a mostly unexplored place, filled with mountain ranges never climbed, trails not hiked, peaks not conquered, and valleys never seen ... . I was able to see more clearly the map of my interior ... . My silent retreat was the direct result of a soul experiencing the crowdedness of self, the emptiness of self, the dead-end of self-absorption. How could I think about God when thoughts about God have to sneak into the few places where I am not thinking about me? When all I do is think about myself, then I am God. And when I am God, where does God go? I discovered in my days of silence that because God is God, He is able to penetrate Himself in the crowded space of my ego. It became clear that God not only makes Himself known He gives me a choice: either worship the God of the mountain or the mountain of yourself, one or the other, but you cannot do both. I also learned something else—giving up the god of myself doesn't happen after a few days of silence or a few books on the inner life or a few hours with a spiritual director. The transfer of worship does not happen after a skirmish on the outskirts of my soul. No, self-absorption does not die easily."[x]

Douglas Southhall Freeman wrote what many consider as the finest biography on General Robert E. Lee, commander in Chief of the Confederate troops during the Civil War. In describing the greatness of Robert E. Lee, Freeman zeroes in on General Lee's extraordinary self-denial and humility. Freeman ends his biography with these words:

> Of humility and submission was born a spirit of self-denial that prepared him for the hardships of war and, still more, for the dark destitution that followed it ... . Had his life been epitomized in one sentence of the Book he read so often, it would have been in the words, "If any man will come after me, let him deny himself, and take up his cross daily, and follow me."
>
> And if one, only one, of all the myriad incidents of his stirring life had to be selected to typify his message, as a man to the young Americans who stood in hushed awe that rainy October morning as their parents wept at the

passing of the Southern Arthur, who would hesitate in selecting that incident?

It occurred in Northern Virginia, probably on his last visit there. A young mother brought her baby to him to be blessed. He took the infant in his arms and looked at it and then at her and slowly said, "Teach him he must deny himself"[xi]

Jesus said, "Blessed are those who hunger and thirst for righteousness, for they shall be satisfied" (Matt. 5:6).

In a culture awash in self-absorption and indulgence, guide us, Lord Jesus, down the path of self-abandonment. We are hungry and thirsty for eternal realities. Teach us, Lord Jesus, your grace and truth.

In Jesus' name we pray, Amen!

Questions

Why has the discipline of fasting often been neglected in recent church history? *Because of the two extremes - overly exalting it + totally ignoring it.*

How did Jesus model the discipline of fasting? *emphasized Embraced it, Endorsed it taught proper motives humility, used Scripture - went off by Himself, for strengthening*

What is the significance of Jesus fasting for forty days in the wilderness before launching his public ministry? *The H.S. was strengthening Jesus Obtaining Spiritual Nourishment so He could withstand Satan's physical att*

What does Tom mean when he states, "When we fast from physical food, we feast on God's word?" *The time we would have Spent on eating we Spend on getting spiritual nourishment.*

What does Jesus teach about fasting in the "Sermon on the Mount?" (See Matthew 6:16-18) *To do it, in secret - put on a normal appearance*

Using Isaiah 58: 3-11 as a biblical backdrop, what are two primary dangers Tom sees in fasting? *If becomes a way to get something rather than a way we get to know God. It becomes a ritualistic form.*

What are two primary delights of fasting?
1. *shatters shackles of enslavement + prides - helps us to be humble*
2. *enhances intimacy w/ God*

How does fasting address the soul tyranny of self-absorption? *It sensitizes us to the needs of others.*

How does Tom suggest we get started in the discipline of fasting? *Start small, ask others who have done well w/ it,*
   Do a Bible Study on Fasting,
   Read a good book on fasting

9

The Smooth Stone of Service

For it is by free grace that you are saved through faith. And this is not of yourselves, but it is the gift of God; Not because of works, lest any man should boast, For we are God's handiwork, recreated in Christ Jesus, that we may do those good works which God predestined for us, that we should walk in them. Ephesians 2:8-10

I will never forget those moments in the hospital when I held Schaeffer and Sarah in my arms for the first time. Nor will I forget the moment I saw my bride, Liz, walk down the isle to meet me on our wedding day. God's goodness absolutely overwhelmed me.

At other times, unforgettable moments are imbedded in sorrow. I will never forget as a young boy placing a rose on my father's casket and watching it being lowered into the cold, dark earth. I'll never forget the time a relationship with a close friend was abruptly severed. Sorrow and grief ambushed me with unrelenting vengeance.

Still other times, unforgettable moments are the fodder for laughter. I will never forget when, shortly after moving into our neighborhood, our two-year-old son decided to shed his clothes and test his urinating skills on the driveway in full view of the entire cul-de-sac. And how could I forget my first visit to a college sweetheart's home when I tried to cut my overcooked pork chop and sent it flying across the dining room.

Unforgettable moments—whether they are filled with inexpressible joy, stinging sorrow or stunning embarrassment—shape us and make us. They also teach us some of life's greatest lessons.

For the disciples, the three years they spent with Jesus contained many unforgettable moments. How about that moment when Jesus spoke to the raging sea and it instantly calmed; or when Jesus took a couple of loaves and fishes and fed five thousand people. Who could forget that moment when Jesus stood outside Lazarus' tomb and cried out, "Come forth" and Lazarus toddled out of the tomb.

Let's examine what I believe was one of the most unforgettable and most shaping moments in the disciples' lives. This unforgettable moment occurred in an upper room shortly before Jesus' crucifixion.

A Lesson in Jesus

In John 13, where Jesus celebrated the Passover meal with his disciples, John painted a compelling picture of an unforgettable moment.

> *Jesus, knowing that the Father had given all things into His hands and that He had come forth from God and was going back to God, rose from supper and laid aside His garments; and taking a towel, He girded Himself about. Then He poured water into the basin and began to wash the disciples' feet and to wipe them with the towel with which He*

was girded. And so He came to Simon Peter, who said to Him, "Lord, do You wash my feet?"

Jesus answered and said to him, "What I do you do not realize now, but you shall understand hereafter."

Peter said to Him, "Never shall You wash my feet!"

Jesus answered him, "If I do not wash you, you have no part with Me."

Simon Peter said to Him, "Lord, not my feet only, but also my hands and my head."

Jesus said to him, "He who has bathed needs only to wash his feet, but is completely clean; and you are clean, but not all of you."

For He knew the one who was betraying Him; for this reason He said, "Not all you are clean."

And so when He had washed their feet and taken His garments and reclined at the table again, He said to them, "Do you know what I have done to you? You call me Teacher (Rabbi) and Lord; and you are right, for so I am. If I then, the Lord and Teacher (Rabbi) washed your feet, you also ought to wash one another's feet. For I gave you an example that you also should do as I did to you. Truly, truly, I say to you, a slave is not greater than his master; neither is one who is sent greater than the one who sent him. If you know these things, you are blessed if you do them."

John 13:3-17

In painting this picture, John, under the Holy Spirit's inspiration, employed two broad literary brush strokes.

Jesus Engages in an Unforgettable Action

In verses three through the first half of verse 12, Jesus absolutely stunned His disciples, not merely by his profound rhetoric, but by His startling actions.

I love the story of the student who, in going to college, pestered his parents about his need for a car. His parents balked, but agreed they would consider getting him a car if he kept his nose clean, cut his long hair, and pulled good grades. After the first semester the son arrived home, proudly showed dad and mom his excellent grades, and said, "Now can I get my car?"

His parents looked at his disheveled condition and his very long hair and said, "Well son, we are excited about your grades, but look at you, and look at your long hair."

Stunned by his parents' response, the college student objected, "But Mom and Dad, Jesus had long hair!"

His father looked him dead in the eye and said, "Yes, Son, and Jesus walked everywhere he went."

In Jesus' day, people walked in open sandals just about everywhere they went, and as a result I imagine their feet became very dirty and smelly. The task reserved for the most menial servant in the first century was washing the dirty feet of guests who arrived at someone's home. In that culture you did not sit in chairs around a table to eat. Rather, you sat on pillows with your feet curled back around you. Dirty, sweaty feet would have been impossible to hide.

John did not tell us why no one had washed the feet of Jesus and his disciples before they entered the upper room for the Passover meal. Perhaps no servant was available to do such a lowly task. But we can infer from the text that the disciples were not about to wash anyone's feet. The implication is that such menial service was below them. When Jesus gathered His disciples for the Last Supper, Luke tells us the disciples were focused on themselves. In fact they were arguing over who was the greatest (Luke 9:46).

In verse three, John reminded us just who this person picking up the basin and towel really was. The irony is gripping. The very God who had made their feet was now washing their feet. Jesus' full deity is emphasized and enhances the full force of Jesus' culturally unthinkable action. The disciples would have never dreamed that the Messiah would do such a thing. Jesus' actions stunned them. Only Peter demonstrated his adroit skill of putting his foot into his mouth.

An Unforgettable Moment in Jerusalem

One of my truly unforgettable moments in life was when I was on a crowded bus in downtown Jerusalem. It was Friday afternoon, and the Jewish Shabat was nearing. Everyone seemed to be out making last minute preparations for the Sabbath. When Liz and I got on the bus, we thought it was crowded, but we managed to find a seat. However, at each stop the number of bodies in the bus grew. We were jammed armpit to armpit, like a bunch of packed sardines.

At one stop, an elderly lady loaded down with packages pushed her way onto the bus and stumbled in our direction. My heart flooded with compassion. I thought, "This lady needs the seat a lot more than you do, Tom."

I was tired enough to resist the benevolent thought for just a moment. Then I stood and motioned for this elderly lady to sit down. I wasn't prepared for what happened next. It was as if a riot was ready to erupt on the bus. With all of the Middle

Eastern emotion they could muster, the people on the bus began to shake their fingers and scream at me. I was frozen in fear! I felt I had become the ignition switch of a highly combustible international incident.

Thankfully, Liz figured out what was going on and told me to sit down. The moment I sat, the storm of protest subsided and the bus returned to normalcy.

What had happened? In giving deference to this older woman, I was committing a cultural taboo. In that cultural situation, men do not defer to women. My unthinkable act resulted in an eruption of cultural outrage. Needless to say, I learned a memorable lesson that afternoon. I wasn't about to do that again!

My experience in a crowded bus in Jerusalem must have reflected the shock the disciples felt at Passover. In picking up the basin and towel, Jesus smashed cultural boundaries and reinforced a timeless spiritual truth. Through an unforgettable action, Jesus gave a sermon no less profound and impacting than the Sermon on the Mount. In the upper room with his disciples, Jesus gave them and us "The sermon of the basin and towel."

Jesus Teaches an Unforgettable Lesson

After Jesus finished washing the disciples' smelly feet, Jesus said to His stunned, and now teachable, disciples, "Do you know what I have done?" Then in verses 13-17, Jesus summoned his disciples to a lifestyle of humble service. One of the marks of the true disciple of Jesus is a life devoted to the basin and towel, a life committed to the discipline of service.

Jesus raised the basin and towel to a whole new level of importance in verses 34-35 when he said, "A new commandment I give to you, that you love one another, even as I have loved you, that you love one another. By this will all men know you are my disciples if you have love for one another."

What was Jesus saying? He was saying that His true followers live lives of sacrificial service to others. The love Jesus speaks about is not gushy and sentimental, but a sacrificial love evidenced by commitment to service. This life pivots not on the hinges of self-absorption, but on self-abandoned service to others.

I'm sure Jesus didn't feel like washing his disciples' feet. Nor was this particularly convenient for Him. But Jesus humbled himself and picked up the towel.

The Apostle Paul reflected on Jesus' modeling of servanthood when he reminded the Philippian believers to embrace the spiritual discipline of service, "Have this attitude in yourselves which was also in Christ Jesus, who although He existed in the form of God, did not regard equality with God a thing to be grasped, but emptied Himself, taking the form of a bond-servant, and being made in the likeness of man. And being found in appearance as a man, He humbled Himself by becoming obedient to the point of death, even death on a cross" (Phil. 2:5-8).

The discipline of service calls us to empty ourselves. Jesus captured this truth in His earthly mission statement when He said, "The Son of Man did not come to be served, but to serve and to give His life a ransom for many" (Matthew 20:28).

In John 13, we are given a vivid and unforgettable picture of a towel. The towel was to be a timeless symbol of a transcendent truth. Just as the cross is the sign of submission, the towel is the sign of service. The fact that the towel has lost its symbolic presence within the Christian community speaks loudly of our being absorbed by the broader, narcissistic culture.

Observing a Humble Servant

I have many precious memories of my wedding day. I will never forget seeing Liz, my beautiful bride, walk down the aisle. Many times I have rehearsed every detail of that special day in my mind, savoring each memory. I don't remember much of what the pastor said, but I do remember what I saw him do earlier in the morning. We had to stop by the church early on Saturday morning. I opened the sanctuary door and peeked inside. Our pastor was on his knees vacuuming the altar area, making sure everything was perfect for our wedding that night. What a lasting lesson our pastor taught us the morning of our wedding! He modeled the discipline of service. He figuratively picked up the basin and the towel.

"The discipline of service is engaging oneself for the good of others with no regard to what the reward will be."[i] The discipline of service involves the reality of personal sacrifice. Jesus said, "Greater love has no one than this, than one lay down his life for his friend" (John 15:13). Jesus is not just referring to the ultimate heroic act of self-sacrifice, but to daily giving our lives in service to others. When we engage in the discipline of service, we lay down our time, our energies, and our resources for another's benefit, without considering what we might receive. Our service to others is not limited by the perimeters of feeling, convenience, or spiritual giftedness, but by our love for God.

Closely related to the discipline of service is the discipline of secrecy. In the discipline of secrecy we refrain from letting our good deeds be known. The discipline of secrecy keeps the motivation for service pure. True service is masked in obscurity. Richard Foster notes, "More than any other single way, the grace of humility is worked in our lives through service."[ii]

The discipline of service is not only a pathway to humility, but also the road to true freedom. Eugene Peterson writes, "The Christian is a person who recognizes that our real problem is not in achieving freedom but in learning service under a better master ... . A servant Christian is the freest person on earth."[iii]

Perhaps the church of Jesus Christ has forgotten that service is a distinguishing mark of authentic Christianity. Like our Lord Jesus, our mission is not to be served, but to serve and give our lives to others. The discipline of service has fallen on hard times. Service is a big deal if someone else is serving us. The table is much more appealing than the towel. To be served is one thing, to serve is quite another. Everybody wants great service, but few want to serve greatly.

The Challenge of Service

The discipline of service has never been easy for me. One summer our family went to Black Mountain North Carolina for a Fellowship of Christian Athletes camp. I had never been to a FCA camp before and was excited to see how it all came together. The leaders told me they would find a job for me to do, and I, in typical pastoral response, said, "I'll be glad to serve in any way I can."

I must admit when I learned my job was working at the camp store, I wasn't excited. I found myself thinking through my resume, "I'm a pastor, I'm a teacher. I have advanced degrees. I have almost twenty years of full-time ministry experience, and I'm going to sell T-shirts to hundreds of teenagers all week? This is not where my spiritual gifts lie; I should be speaking; I should be teaching."

Yet God didn't want me to teach anyone that week. He had

a tailor-made lesson just for me to learn. It was a lesson about service. I wanted to be on stage using my gifts; God wanted me in the camp store developing my servanthood. As I worked in that camp store, this thought ran through my mind, "Tom, you are never more pleasing to Me than when you are serving others."

Often my greatest insights have not come from times of visibility, but rather obscurity. My life has been transformed the most, not from times of speaking, but from times of serving. How I thank God for the ministry of the towel!

Often we rationalize our unwillingness to pick up the towel. We just don't have enough time to serve our spouse. We are too busy to serve a neighbor or a friend. Or we try to convince ourselves that we don't have the spiritual gift of helps or mercy. Or we think, "Let's find someone else in the church to do this, and pay them if we need to."

Not long ago I ran across this little poem:

I'll Go Where You Want Me To Go-Maybe
I'll go where you want me to go, dear Lord,
Real service is what I desire.
I'll sing a solo any time, dear Lord.
But don't ask me to sing in the choir.

I'll do what you want me to do, dear Lord,
I like to see things come to pass.
But don't ask me to teach boys and girls, O Lord.
I'd rather stay in my class.

I'll do what you want me to do, dear Lord,
I yearn for thy kingdom to thrive.
I'll give you my nickels and dimes, dear Lord.
But please don't ask me to tithe.

I'll go where you want me to go, dear Lord.
I'll say what you want me to say.
I'm busy just now myself, dear Lord,
So I'll help you some other day.iv
[Author unknown]

A Compelling Plea to Make a Life Changing Decision

One of the most profound and damaging affects of our material affluence is that we order our lives around the consumption of things, rather than caring for people. This consumer mindset creeps into the church.

Too often we approach our involvement and local church commitment on the basis of what we get out of it, rather than focusing on what we give to it. We are tempted to be spectators of the religious show rather than diligent servants of the King. We sit in the stands instead of joining the team working on the field.

We place value on our church experience based on whether or not we get something out of the worship service, or whether or not our children get excited about their experience. In our minds we have a rating system for the various programs of the church. When a program does not live up to our expectations, rather than rolling up our sleeves and becoming part of the solution, we search for someone else to take that position.

The church is to work hard at meeting needs, but it is not to be a reflection of a consumer culture—it is to be Christ's bride. We are called to worship the Living God, not simply consume religious products. Few things are more toxic to authentic Christian community than self-absorbed consumerism.

The discipline of service is the antidote to the deadly poison of consumerism. Each of us must pick up the smooth stone of service. The church of Jesus Christ must once again pick up the towel. Our professional slickness is not what gives us credibility with the postmodern world—our credibility comes from our humble service offered in Christ's name. Jesus reminds us that the humility of our service is an important apologetic for the truthfulness of the gospel message. We must cast aside our obsession with self and embrace the discipline of service.

How To Embrace the Smooth Stone of Service

Choosing the Lesser Place

Rather than seeking a place of prominence so we can receive praise, true Christ-followers look for places of obscurity in which to serve people. Dietrich Bonhoeffer observes, "The second service that one should perform for another in a Christian community is that of active helpfulness. This means, initially, simple assistance in trifling, external matters. There is a multitude of these things wherever people live together. Nobody is too good for the meanest service. One who worries about the loss of time that such petty, outward acts of helpfulness entail is usually taking the importance of his own career too seriously."[v]

Picking Up the Basin and the Towel

When we put on the yoke of Christ, we pick up the basin and the towel. At this point, we are making the life-changing decision to become a true servant. This requires a radical re-orientation of our time and priorities. It changes our marriages, our approach to church, and even our approach to work.

Many of us would like to serve others, but do not have the

time or emotional and financial margin. Rather than sinking into a morass of guilt, let's be courageous enough and committed enough to take the necessary steps to build margin into our life. This may mean dramatically changing our lifestyles. It may mean adjusting a standard of living. It may lead to a career change. Picking up the basin and towel will require bold adjustments.

Picking up the Basin and Towel Means We Place a Higher Value on Local Church Community

Because God places such high value on the local church, we must also do so. Some of us have been hurt or disillusioned from church experiences. We have seen the church's shortcomings. Our idealism has been shattered. Some us have seen the church as irrelevant and are just now rediscovering its importance.

Whatever our feelings about the local church, let's remember the church is God's primary tool to build His kingdom. Our church family is an important place for each one of us to serve. Look for needs within your church fellowship and take the initiative to meet them. Don't wait for someone else to respond. Don't just write a check to pay someone else to get the job done. Roll up your sleeves and humbly serve.

Experts who evaluate the local church refer to the 80/20 rule, which states that in a typical church, about 20 percent of the people serve and give while 80 percent primarily watch. In other words, two out of 10 pull the load, and eight out of 10 enjoy the ride.

This is not God's design for the church. Could this be one reason why the local church is often so ineffective? I can't imagine the Kansas City Chief's football team having a winning record if only 20 percent of their players played the game. Let's renew our commitment to serve well in the spiritual community we call home.

We Must Teach Our Children the Discipline of Service

As a child and then as a teenager, few things impacted me more than seeing my mother model the discipline of service in my home, my church, and our community. I didn't need a sermon to tell me that authentic Christianity and service were inseparable. Husbands and wives, model the discipline of service to your children by serving one another, serving your neighbors, and serving the needy. Involve your children in service. One way our family loves to serve is to prepare meals in an inner city food pantry on Thanksgiving Day. We can find many ways to serve others in our neighborhoods and in our cities. Teach your children to serve without expecting financial reward. Teach them to serve in secret for the glory of God and for the wholeness of their souls.

A Thanksgiving Day editorial in the newspaper told of a schoolteacher who asked her class of first graders to draw a picture of what they were most thankful for. She thought of how little these children from poor neighborhoods had to be thankful for. But she knew most of them would draw pictures of turkeys or food-laden tables. The teacher was startled by the picture Douglas handed in—it was a childishly drawn hand.

But whose hand was it? The class was captivated. "I think it must be the hand of God that brings us food," said one child.

"A farmer," said another, "because he grows the turkeys."

Finally the teacher bent over Douglas's desk and asked whose hand it was. "It's your hand, Teacher," he mumbled.[vi]

Practicing God's Presence

We must once again embrace the truth that all of our work is to be an offering to God. The Apostle Paul writes, "Whatever you do, do all to the glory of God"(1 Cor. 10:31). Acts of service whether in the workplace, the church, our neighborhood, or in our homes are to be altars of worship.

A great man in Christian history was simply referred to as Brother Lawrence. Desiring to follow Jesus Christ, he entered the discipline of humble service. In the kitchen of a monastery, slaving over a hot stove, Brother Lawrence learned his greatest lessons of faith. In his classic work, *Practicing The Presence of God,* Brother Lawrence writes, "The time of business, does not with me differ from the time of prayer; and in the noise and clatter of my kitchen, while several persons are at the same time calling for different things; I possess God in as great tranquility as if I were upon my knees."[vii]

Closing Thoughts

I don't often read the airline's magazine when I'm sitting on a plane, but recently an article captivated my interest. Under the headline "Making A Difference" was a large picture of Millard Fuller. The article began with these words, "At age 29, Alabama lawyer and businessman Millard Fuller was a millionaire, and he put a pretty fancy roof over his head. But within a few years, he and wife Linda said good-bye to all that and started putting modest roofs over the heads of the poor."

The article described the remarkable impact this decision is making in our world. Fuller founded Habitat for Humanity, which now works in all 50 U.S. states and 57 other countries with building or renovating 34 houses each day. Habitat built 10,000 houses in its first 15 years; it expects to build 13,000 in 1998 alone.

In the article, Millard Fuller was asked what inspired him to begin Habitat For Humanity. Fuller responded, "Following a marital crisis, my wife and I reconciled, and out of that came a decision to divest ourselves of wealth and seek a path of service as Christians. We literally went looking for a way to have our lives count for God's work in the world."[viii]

A heart overflowing with Christ has hands filled with service! Oh, the lasting legacy of the basin and the towel!

Nathan Schaeffer in his book *Quotable Quotations* wrote, "At the close of life, the question will be not how much you have got, but how much you have given. Not how much you have won, but how much have you done. Not how much you have saved, but how much you have sacrificed. It will be how much you have loved and served, not how much you have been honored!"[ix]

Lord Jesus, forgive me for my self-absorption. Teach me to pick up the basin and towel of humble service to others. Guard my heart from wanting to be recognized by others for my good deeds. Guide me in the narrow path of a quiet obscurity. Amen

Questions

Tom suggests that Jesus' unthinkable actions recorded in John 13 were one of the most unforgettable moments in the disciples three years with Jesus. Do you agree? Disagree? Why?

I agree. The fact that no one had ever done it is huge. What a major impact. He totally rearranged their thinking preparing them for the What was coming.

What does the disciples' unwillingness to wash each other's feet indicate about their cultural and spiritual blindness?

They didn't get the servanthood idea at all.

What lesson(s) was Jesus trying to teach His disciples by washing their dirty feet?

1. To put others first 2. No job is too menial 3. Servanthood is of utmost importance

In what areas do we have cultural and spiritual blindness that hinder us from living the abundant life in Jesus' kingdom?

In thinking that "I would never do that ...."

What is meant by the discipline of service?

Self abandoned service to others Sacrificial love evidenced by by commitment to service"

How is the discipline of service related to humility? (Comment on Philippians 2:1-11)

Because service "calls us to empty ourselves"

How does the discipline of service serve as an antidote to the religious consumerism so prevalent within the church?

Because instead of focusing on what we get we focus on what we give

What does "choosing the lesser place" mean?

Looking for a place of obscurity to serve others.

Tom observes, "A heart overflowing with Christ has hands filled with service." What are some ways you can begin to pick up the basin and towel in your family, your workplace, and the church?

Works/ Acts/ Deeds of Service small & large.

10

Engaging the Sling of Faith

Now faith is the assurance the confirmation, the title deed) of the things [we] hope for, being the proof of things [we] do not see and the conviction of reality [faith perceiving as real fact what is not revealed to the sense]. Hebrews 11:1

A couple of months after our wedding, my wife and I moved to Dallas, Texas. We had been asked to give leadership direction to the Campus Crusade for Christ ministry at Southern Methodist University. We packed all our earthly belongings in a Ryder moving truck and, with great expectation, headed to Texas. However, we had one significant problem—we had no place to live.

We had tried to find a home. All through the summer several friends had searched for affordable housing near the SMU campus for us, but had found nothing. Dallas's economic boom at that time left housing a pricey and rare commodity. With the school year quickly approaching and our staff team waiting, we knew we had to be in Dallas, but where would we live?

Thankfully, my wife's father, who lived in Dallas, was kind enough to let us stay a few days with him, so we parked our Ryder truck at his house and looked frantically for housing. My frustration level rose. I began wrestling with God. Our conversation went something like this, "God, you know that I am not single anymore; I can't just live anywhere. You know we have done everything we can to find a place close to SMU. You called us to lead this ministry, so what am I supposed to do? Have You led us here only to let us down?"

In spite of our anguish, my wife and I kept looking. Finally, we found a suitable apartment a long distance from SMU. As we were filling out forms at the leasing agent's office, she received a phone call. Much to her surprise and ours, the phone call was for us! She handed the phone to me, and I spoke with a friend who had been looking for a place for us all summer. He asked if we had already signed the lease. When I told him we were about to, he insisted, "Don't sign it; I think I found the perfect place for you. It is a condo right across from the SMU campus."

We excused ourselves from the agent's office and bolted out of the door, racing for the SMU campus. When we arrived at the address, our hearts began to leap. Our friend was with a dear lady who owned two condominiums next to SMU. Both her sons had been tennis players at the university, and now one of them had moved away. She apologized for the messy state of the condominium, but emphasized that if it would work for us, she would be delighted to lease it to us at an affordable price.

When we walked into the condominium, we drooled. The fully furnished condominium had a perfect layout for entertaining students. Liz loved the colors and décor! Being newly married, we had little furniture and here we were being offered a fully furnished, spacious condominium at a great price! Patches of Godlight suddenly filled that condominium! At that moment we all knew that God had reserved this special place just for us to enjoy and minister to students. When our circumstances had looked bleakest, God had provided for us beyond our wildest dreams.

This unforgettable experience carved into my heart a life-transforming truth. Kingdom faith often does not have a contingency plan, just a desperate dependence on God.

When the young shepherd boy stood before mammoth Goliath, David didn't have a contingency plan! David placed himself in a position of desperate dependence on God. He had no plan B! When David picked up the sling, he entered the kingdom faith zone. While the five smooth stones represent, for me, the spiritual disciplines of the wilderness, the sling used to propel the stones represents the transforming faith that God desires for us who pursue the path to wholeness of soul. God uses our faith in Him and our spiritual discipline to create a powerful kingdom synergy for accomplishing His sovereign purposes.

In examining the "sling of faith," I would like to probe a foundational question, discover three life-changing principles, and offer three brief reminders for us to take with us in our journey of faith.

What Is Authentic Faith?

Faith is a commonly used word, but what is it, really? The Bible speaks much about faith and devotes an entire chapter to what some theologians refer to as the hall of faith. In Hebrews 11, we are ushered into God's hall of champions. Much like the football hall of fame in Canton, Ohio, or the baseball hall of fame in Cooperstown, New York or the NCAA hall of champions in Indianapolis, Indiana, display after display of scripture recalls the timeless glories of these great champions of faith.

In our exuberance to enjoy the inspiring hall of faith in Hebrews chapter 11, we often rush past the first few verses. This is perilous; for here we discover what authentic faith really is! Beginning at the end of Hebrews 10 and continuing to chapter 11, we read, "But we are not of those who shrink back to destruction, but of those who have faith to the preserving of the soul. Now faith is the assurance of things hoped for, the conviction of things not seen. For by it the men of old gained approval. By faith we understand the worlds were prepared by the word of God, so that what is seen was not made out of things which are visible."

The chapter break here does us a bit of disservice. Chapter breaks often create the illusion of discontinuity when the continuity of thought is really very close. For 10:39 reminds us that we must have authentic faith for true wholeness of soul.

What is this authentic faith? In Hebrews 11:1-3, we get a vastly different understanding of faith than in the crippling caricatures of our culture. Today, faith is most often portrayed as a blind, subjective, mystical leap into irrationality. The *Star Wars Trilogy* gave us the enlightened "Yoda," whose mystical faith in the "force" exhibited extraordinary powers. Luke, his young protégé, was urged to bypass rational thought and jump into the mystical abyss of "using the force."

In the *Indiana Jones* movies staring Harrison Ford, faith is also portrayed as a blind, subjective, mystical leap into irrationality. In his quest for the Holy Grail, Indiana Jones, facing an insurmountable distance over a bottomless abyss, closes his eyes and steps into the unknown.

Another crippling caricature is portraying faith as a soothing psychological crutch. This is a resilient legacy of Sigmund Freud, who understood religious faith to be an irrational security blanket for the weak.

I often find myself in the wake of this wave of thought in the fast moving current of our culture. I usually hear it in the condescending tone of "Well Tom, if that faith thing works for you that's great."

But what does God's Word say authentic faith really is all about? Is it merely a subjective, blind leap into the dark unknown? Is faith merely a soothing security blanket? Or is it something vastly different?

In Hebrews 11:1 we read, "Now faith is the assurance of things hoped for, the conviction of things not seen." When we see the English word "hope," we attach to it the idea of an idealistic possibility. For example, we often say, "She only had a hope and a prayer."

But this is different than the meaning of the original language in this text. A more literal translation of this verse is this: "Faith is the foundational essence of all confidence." We often think that sensory perception, rather than faith perception, is the foundational essence of confidence. If we can see it, smell it, and touch it, we figure it's real. But if we cannot, its reality is suspect. We are told faith is trusting in something you cannot see, but this is really to conceal the full meaning of biblical faith. Authentic faith is not so much trusting in what you cannot see, as it is seeing what many fail to see.

Recently, I struggled with a respiratory bug that knocked me out. I went to bed and crashed. The next morning when I came downstairs, Sarah, knowing I wasn't feeling well, tried to give me a positive greeting. She said, "Dad, you look better, and you smell better." I am sure my daughter, looking at me, had great sensory perception!

The word translated "conviction" in verse one was used to describe "compelling evidence and incontrovertible facts in a court of law." By using this word, what does the biblical author assert? Authentic faith is anything but a blind leap into irrationality or a psychological crutch—it is the foundational substance of reality.

What then is authentic faith? Authentic faith is the foundational essence of true confidence, a core substance of reality.

Verse three further reinforces this understanding of authentic faith. Authentic faith in God and His revealed word is the keyhole into which we can peer and see a glimpse of true reality—a keyhole made possible through God's revealed Word. This window of authentic faith allows us to discern that God's Word is the creative cause of the entire visible universe. In other words, authentic faith is not peripheral to true understanding, it is foundational to all understanding. Faith is not merely a comforting refuge we seek when all other roads of knowledge reach a dead end street. Authentic faith is the foundational road—a faith that is anchored in biblical revelation.

Professor Robert Jastrow, a great astronomer and intellectual, wrote a book titled *God and the Astronomers.* Jastrow understood the foundational role faith plays in acquiring true knowledge. Jastrow writes, "For the scientist who has lived by his faith in the power of reason, the story ends like a bad dream. He has scaled the mountains of ignorance; he is about to conquer the highest peak; as he pulls himself over the final rock, he is greeted by a band of theologians who have been sitting there for centuries."[i]

We often think our sensory perception allows us to discern true reality. However, our faith in Jesus Christ is what lets us peel back the veneer of this fallen and sin stained material realm and glimpse eternity. Journalist Linda Bowles asserted, "A few hundred years ago, the belief was widespread that science would eventually provide all the answers … . Early philosophers speculated that the need for religion would decline as science unraveled the mysteries of the universe. Alas, the opposite has happened. Every new truth opened new doors for inquiry. It is commonly agreed that every time science answers a question, at least two new questions never asked before become possible. Ignorance is expanding at twice the rate of knowledge. By extrapolation, we know relatively less and less about more and more. The deep mysteries of life recede as we approach. There is no end to them, only an unfolding outward and away from our reach."[ii]

Oh, the awesome majesty of our God! Oh, the wonder that fills our souls when we place our faith in God's Word and in His Son Jesus Christ. Though authentic faith is often difficult to precisely define, we can clearly observe its characteristics.

Three Characteristics of Authentic Faith

Authentic Faith Ignites Spiritual Vision

Tucked in an obscure crevice of Scripture is a profound picture of authentic faith igniting spiritual vision. It is the account of Elisha's servant who experienced a watershed moment in his life. Although Elisha's servant believed in God and had seen God work through Elisha, he was locked into this temporal world. He had eyesight, but lacked vision. He only saw Syria's mighty army, and understandably, felt blood-curdling fear! That is, until the veil of temporality was lifted. He then got a small glimpse of God's kingdom. Elisha's servant got the kingdom picture!

In 2 Kings 6:15 we read, "Now when the attendant of the man of God had risen early and gone out, behold an army with horses and chariots was circling the city. And his servant said to

[Elisha], 'Alas, my master! What shall we do?' So he answered, 'Do not fear for those who are with us are more than those who are with them.' Then Elisha prayed and said, 'O Lord I pray, open his eyes that he may see.' And the Lord opened the servant's eyes, and he saw, and behold, the mountain was full of horses and chariots of fire all around Elisha."

Facing overwhelming odds, Elisha's servant froze in fear. Yet we have no indication that Elisha was afraid at all. What was the difference? The difference was authentic faith—a faith that ignited true spiritual vision in the depths of his soul. What a tragedy to have eyesight, but lack true vision! What anguish to be confined to the lower room of this sin stained material realm, when the glories of the upper room beckon the weary pilgrim. Authentic faith is not so much trusting in what you cannot see, rather it is seeing what so many fail to see.

"While we look not at the things which are seen, but at the things which are not seen, for the things which are seen are temporal, but the things that are unseen are eternal," Paul writes in 2 Corinthians 4:18. Authentic faith gives us new spiritual eyesight and lets us see beyond our overwhelming circumstances— whether they be difficult relationships, devastating injustice, or financial hurdles. Elisha's servant learned what we must learn through the eyes of authentic faith, that is, one person with God is a true majority. What matters is not the greatness of our faith, but the greatness of our God. Faith is only as good as the worthiness of the object in which we place our faith.

Few of us would get on an airplane with an engine dangling from the wing, even if the captain tried to persuade us we could still fly. Authentic faith must have a worthy object! Authentic faith ignites our souls with spiritual vision. It also energizes our souls with steadfast courage.

Authentic Faith Energizes Steadfast Courage

Our Lord Jesus in His short time on this earth taught many lessons about faith to his twelve disciples. But perhaps the most memorable was when a fierce storm hit the Sea of Galilee:

"And on that day, when evening had come, He said to them, 'Let us go over to the other side.' And leaving the multitude, they took Him along with them, just as He was, in the boat; and the other boats were with Him. And there arose a fierce gale of wind, and the waves were breaking over the boat so much that the boat was already filling up. And He Himself was in the stern, asleep on the cushion; and they awoke Him and said to Him, 'Teacher, do You not care that we are perishing?' And being aroused, He rebuked the wind and said to the sea, 'Hush, be still.' And the wind died down and it became perfectly calm. And He said to them, 'Why are you so timid? How is it that you have no faith?' And they became very much afraid and said to one another, 'Who then is this, that even the wind and the sea obey Him?'" (Mark 4:35-41)

The disciples, many of them seasoned fishermen, were terrified as this storm raged. Jesus not only calmed the storm with a simple phrase, He also rebuked his disciples for their lack of courage in the storm. Jesus notes that the disciples' timidity was due to their lack of faith. Their lack of faith left them afraid and vulnerable when they faced a sudden, ominous storm!

In this familiar story, we can find a very profound truth. If we are to have the courage to face the storms of this life, our souls must be filled with authentic faith. What life storms are you facing? Is it a turbulent marriage? A broken relationship? The loss of a loved one? A shattered dream? A financial crisis? A prolonged illness?

So often in the midst of the storms of suffering, we cry out to God in fear, "Lord take this away?" And then if God does not calm the storm, we get angry.

Why not cry out in faith to God? Not "Lord, take this away," but rather "Lord, give me the courage to be strong and faithful in the storm." Authentic faith does not cower in the corner of self-pity, but leans into the wind and finds God in the eye of the storm.

Authentic Faith Unleashes Supernatural Power

On our faith journey to authentic spirituality and wholeness of soul, like David, we will encounter giants like Goliath who lurk in the shadows. We'll see giants of anger, lust, greed, bitterness, emptiness, and loneliness! Like David, we must pick up the five smooth stones and engage these giants of the soul with the sling of faith. John reminds us that though we face a powerful foe, "Greater is He who is in us than he who is in the world" (1 John 4:4).

Contrary to the messages we hear every day in our information rich culture, the human soul is not merely a sensual playground—it is a high stakes spiritual battlefield. The most intense cosmic struggle is fought every day on the front lines of the human soul. But John also reminds us that authentic faith in Jesus Christ unleashes the supernatural power we need to live a victorious life. John writes, "For whatever is born of God overcomes the world; and this is the victory that has overcome the world—our faith" (1 John 5:4).

Authentic faith does not carry the white flag of surrender, but lifts up the checkered flag of victory. A victory won for us at the cross of Calvary!

Authentic faith is the spiritual catalyst of the soul—the change agent that transforms us into the likeness of Jesus Christ. The Apostle Paul declared, "I am crucified with Christ, and it is no longer I who live, but Christ lives in me; and the life which I now live in the flesh, I live by faith in the Son of God, who loved me and delivered Himself up for me" (Galatians 2:20).

Three Reminders about Authentic Faith

Faith Embraces Spiritual Discipline

David needed both the smooth stones of discipline and the sling of faith to slay Goliath. Faith training embraces spiritual discipline. Spiritual discipline strengthens and deepens our faith. Spiritual discipline and faith have a synergistic dynamic. "So faith comes from hearing and hearing by the word of Christ," Paul wrote in Romans 10:17. Faith feeds on the truths of God's Word.

Postmodern apologist Ravi Zacharias has observed, "One of the most painful realities I have found in traveling around the globe is the epidemic proportions of indiscipline. Whether it is in our studies or in our habits, we seem to always find the line of least resistance and then blame God when we fail in our commitment to come to Him on His own terms."[iii]

Faith Grows with Exercise

Authentic faith is like a muscle—the more you use it, the stronger it becomes. If your faith is not being exercised, it is atrophying. Maybe your faith is in a rut. One definition of a rut is a shallow grave with both ends hollowed out. The more we learn to walk by faith, the more our souls will possess vision, courage, and power. Are you increasingly able to place yourself in a position of desperate dependence on God?

Faith Propels Us Out of Our Comfort Zones

By its very nature, faith will stretch you and make you feel uncomfortable. Just ask Peter how he felt as he stepped out on the Sea of Galilee. This is what I call real knee-knocking faith.

Knee-knocking faith moves us out of our comfort zones. Knee-knocking faith is not paralyzed by "What if?" but propelled forward by "What now?"

What areas of knee-knocking faith is God calling you to embrace? Maybe for the first time you will need to trust God with your finances by honoring Him with your first fruits. Or perhaps your point of leaving your comfort zone is sharing Christ with a neighbor or friend at work or school. Perhaps God is prompting you to seek reconciliation of a broken relationship. God wants to move you out of your comfort zone and into a faith zone—a place of desperate dependence on Him!

A friend of mine has astutely observed that the cult of the comfortable is the curse of the Christian. God has called us not to comfort, but to faith-inspired obedience. A whole soul is filled with faith, not fear! The writer of Hebrews reminds us, "And without faith it is impossible to please Him, for he who comes to God must believe that He is, and that He is a rewarder of those who seek Him" (Hebrews 11:6).

Lighthouses and Compasses

The Northern shore of Lake Superior is a breathtaking wonder of God's creation with its tall jagged rock cliffs and spectacular waterfalls. On a family vacation to Northern Minnesota recently, we drove along the scenic U.S. Hwy 61. We found many spectacular sights on Minnesota's Northern shore and, yes, many "tourists traps" that continually beckon the curious traveler.

Perhaps the most spectacular landmark is the Split Rock Lighthouse. Perched atop a solid rock cliff, you can see the Split Rock Lighthouse for many miles. Completed by the U.S. Lighthouse Service in 1910, it is restored and operated by the Minnesota Historical Society as a state park.

Like most tourists, our family pulled off Hwy 61 and entered the Split Rock Lighthouse State Park. We love to explore lighthouses, and although we were tired from our journey, a sense of excitement revived our enthusiasm.

Our enthusiasm waned a bit when we discovered that we could not go into the lighthouse until a group tour had finished. Liz and Sarah decided to discover some other views along the cliff, but Schaeffer and I sat down near the lighthouse to rest. Suddenly, a woman who worked at the lighthouse appeared. She enthusiastically blurted out, "Is there anything you want to know about the lighthouse?" Before we could answer, she began to tell us all about the lighthouse's history. At first we listened in an obligatory fashion, but as she began to tell the story of the Split Rock Lighthouse our interest intensified.

She told us that the reason the Split Rock Lighthouse had been built in that location was because so many mining ships had crashed along the rocky shore. Large cargo ships would carry iron ore from Duluth through the Great Lakes to the steel mills in the Eastern United States. Lake Superior often had great storms, but it wasn't just the violence of the storms that ruined the ships, something more insidious lurked under the surface that made the shipping captains lose their way. Something altered their navigational equipment and distorted their compass settings!

What was that something? The large deposits of iron in the rocky cliffs distorted the navigational equipment so their true North readings were off by several degrees. Thus when the ships approached the area where the Split Rock Lighthouse now stands, their navigational equipment wasn't dependable enough for them to avoid the perilous rocky shore. After much loss of life and property—especially after a mighty 1905 November storm—the shipping companies finally figured out the problem and went to Washington D.C., pleading with the government to build a lighthouse.

As I listened, I thought of a spiritual parallel. Many perils line the way for those who desire to follow a path to wholeness of the soul. During most of the journey, if we depend on timeless compass settings of truth, we will be able to navigate quite well. But at times and places in the journey, we also need a lighthouse to guide us through very perilous waters.

In these pages, I have attempted to introduce you to some timeless compass settings that will give you direction for the journey. I have found these timeless compass settings to be biblically sound and psychologically whole!

But may I encourage you to also find a couple of lighthouses to consult during your journey? Seek wise, Christ-like mentors who have journeyed further down the path and have gained some treasured insight.

A wise "lighthouse" once advised me, "Wherever, you go find the most Christ-like people you can find and get in the middle of them." Find a lighthouse! Be a lighthouse for someone else! You'll find great joy in the journey! Shalom!

In conclusion, be strong in the Lord; draw your strength from Him.

Put on God's whole armor, that you may be able successfully

To stand up against [all] the strategies and the deceits of the devil...

Stand therefore, having tightened the belt of truth around your loins

And having put on the breastplate of integrity and of moral rectitude and right standing with God.

And having shod your feet in preparation of the Gospel of peace.

Lift up over all the shield of saving faith, upon which you can quench all the flaming missiles.

And take the helmet of salvation and the sword that the Spirit wields, which is the Word of God.

Pray at all times in the Spirit, with all [manner of] prayer and entreaty.

To that end keep alert and watch with strong purpose and perseverance,

Interceding in behalf of all the saints [God's consecrated people]. Eph. 6: 10-11, 13-18

Questions

How does the Holy Scripture define faith? (See Hebrews 11:1) *Faith is being sure of what we do not see see + the assurance of what we hope for*

What are some of the crippling caricatures we have about faith? *That it is a blind leap - "mystical irrationality + subjective or a soothing psychological crutch*

Comment on Tom's assertion that, "Authentic faith in God and His revealed Word is the keyhole into which we can peer and see a glimpse of true reality." *God's word reveals Himself to us, reveals His ways, confirms our faith teaches us. Through faith we better understand what He is reveal*

What is meant by the myth of certainty? Why is the myth of certainty such a threat to authentic spirituality?

What are three characteristics of authentic faith? *must have a worthy object, ignites souls w/ spiritual vision, energizes w/ steadfast courage unleashes supernat pow*

How have you seen these characteristics woven into the tapestry of your spiritual experience?

Tom gives three brief reminders about authentic faith. Which can you relate to and why? *grows w/ exercise Have to flex the muscle - use it - strengthe it - feels good.*

How does faith grow in the soil of the soul?

What do you think Tom means when he says, "Authentic faith puts us in a posture of a desperate dependence on God?" *Because only when you are showing true faith will you be in a position to truly depend on God all*

When have you found yourself in a position of desperate dependence on God? How did God get you through this situation? *Current - trust*

Footnotes

Chapter 1, Experiencing The Spiritual Birth

i   Elton Trueblood, *A Place To Stand*, page 18.

ii   Literally from above.

iii   Leon Morris, *Commentary*, page 219.

iv   Max Lucado, *He Still Moves Stones*, pages 127-128.

v   Wind and spirit are the same word in the original languages of Holy Scripture.

vi   Dallas Willard, *Spirit of the Disciplines*, page 67.

vii   Blaise Pascal, *Pensee's*, page 285.

Chapter 2, Putting On Jesus' Easy Yoke

i   *48 Hours*, February 4, 1998.

ii   Os Guinness, *The Call*, page 4.

iii   Doug Webster, *The Easy Yoke*, page 11.

iv   Ibid, page 15.

v   Dietrich Bonhoeffer, *The Cost of Discipleship*.

vi   Doug Webster, *The Easy Yoke*, page 85.

vii   Ibid, page 169.

Chapter 3, Shedding Saul's Armor

i Gary Richmond, *A View From the Zoo,* pages 24-27.

Chapter 4, Picking Up The Five Smooth Stones

i Gordon McDonald, *The Life God Blesses,* pages xx-xxiii.

ii Allan Loy McGinnis, *The Friendship Factor,* pages 60-61.

iii Quoted in Culwell's prayer letter.

iv Gordon McDonald, *The Life God Blesses,* page 42.

v Vern Lunquist, 1998 Winter Olympics, CBS, February, 20, 1998.

vi Eugene Petersen, *A Long Obedience in the Same Direction,* page 12. Also quoted in Charles Swindoll's *Seasons of Life,* page 47.

vii Mark McMinn, *Psychology, Theology & Spirituality,* page 143.

Chapter 5, The Smooth Stone of Solitude

i From D. Min. Notes, pages 11 and 161.

ii Jeanne Guyon, *Experiencing The Depths Of Jesus Christ,* page 108.

iii Henry David Thoreau, *On Walden Pond,* page 107.

iv Dallas Willard, *Spirit of the Disciplines,* page 161.

v Quoted in "Disciplines for the Inner life," page 64, from *With Christ in the School Of Prayer.*

vi Gordon McDonald, *The Life God Blesses,* page 190.

vii Christian Research Institute's letter, August 15, 1995.

viii Gordon McDonald, *The Life God Blesses,* page 28.

ix Ibid, pages 225-226.

Chapter 6, The Smooth Stone of Prayer

i   Dr. Peter Wagner, *Prayer Shield,* page 79.

ii   Dallas Willard, *Spirit of the Disciplines,* page 186.

iii   William Carey, *Celebration of Discipline,* page 30.

iv   Bill Hybels, *Too Busy Not To Pray,* page 7.

v   Ben Patterson, *Deepening Your Conversation with God,* page 51.

vi   William Carey, *Celebration of Discipline,* pages 34-35.

vii   John White, *Daring To Draw Near,* page 14.

viii   William Law, *A Serious Call To A Devout And Holy Life,* page 91.

Chapter 7, The Smooth Stone of Study

i   Dr. Mark Noll, *The Scandal of The Evangelical Mind,* page 4.

ii   Dr. David Wells, *God in The Wasteland,* page 118.

iii   Dr. Mark Noll, *The Scandal of The Evangelical Mind,* pg. 26

iv   Dr. David Wells, *No Place for Truth,* page 180.

v   A.W. Tozer, *Knowledge of the Holy,* page 9.

vi   Ravi Zacharias, *Cries of The Heart,* page 46.

vii   William Law, *A Serious Call To a Devout and Holy Life,* page 153.

viii   *The Elisabeth Elliot Newsletter,* March/April 1998.

ix   Dietrich Bonhoeffer, *Life Together,* page 45.

x   Blaise Pascal, *Penses,* page 229.

xi   Quoted in Ravi Zacharias,' *Can Man Live Without God?,* page 43.

xii   *Time,* November 15, 1993, page 75.

Chapter 8, The Smooth Stone of Fasting

i   Richard Foster, *Celebration of Discipline*, page 41.

ii   "Finding Spirituality On a Path of Fasting," *The Kansas City Star*, March 11, 1998.

iii   Aruthur Wallis, *God's Chosen Fast*, page 9.

iv   Richard Foster, *Celebration of Discipline*, page 41.

v   *Chicken Soup for the Soul*, page 73.

vi   Dr. Bill Bright, *The Coming Revival*, page 97.

vii   Dallas Willard, *Spirit of the Disciplines*, page 166.

viii   John Piper, *A Hunger For God*, Chapter 4.

ix   Bill Bright, *The Coming Revival*, page 93.

x   Mike Yaconelli, "Self-evaluation or Self-absorption?," *The Wittenberg Door*, October, 1995.

xi   Quoted in Charles Swindoll's *Living Above The Level Of Mediocrity*, page 54.

Chapter 9, The Smooth Stone of Service

i   Dallas Willard, class notes.

ii   Richard Foster, *Celebration of Discipline*, page 113.

iii   Eugene Peterson, *A Long Obedience In The Same Direction*, pages 61and 64.

iv   Speakers Sourcebook, page 223.

v   Dietrich Bonhoeffer, *Life Together*, page 99.

vi   *Chicken Soup for the Soul*, page 133.

vii   *The Treasury of Spiritual Classics*, page 570.

viii   United Airline's *Hemispheres* magazine, March 1998, pages 16 and 18.

ix   Nathan C. Schaeffer, *Quotable Quotations,* page 350.

Chapter 10, Engaging The Sling of Faith

i   Quoted in *Intellectuals Speak Out About God,* page 138, from *God and The Astronomers.*

ii   The *Kansas City Star,* April 8, 1998.

iii   Ravi Zacharias, *Cries of the Heart,* page 6.